D1595744

VAN CORTLANDT

Family Papers

VOLUME ONE

THE HUDSON RIVER VALLEY c. 1776

An architect and surveyor by training, Claude Joseph Sauthier, who drew the original of the map (over), was born in Strasbourg in 1736. He came to the North American colonies around 1768, and was a cartographer for Governor William Tryon of North Carolina. When that official was transferred to New York in 1771, Sauthier accompanied him. The original of this particular map of the Hudson River was engraved in London in 1776 by William Faden.

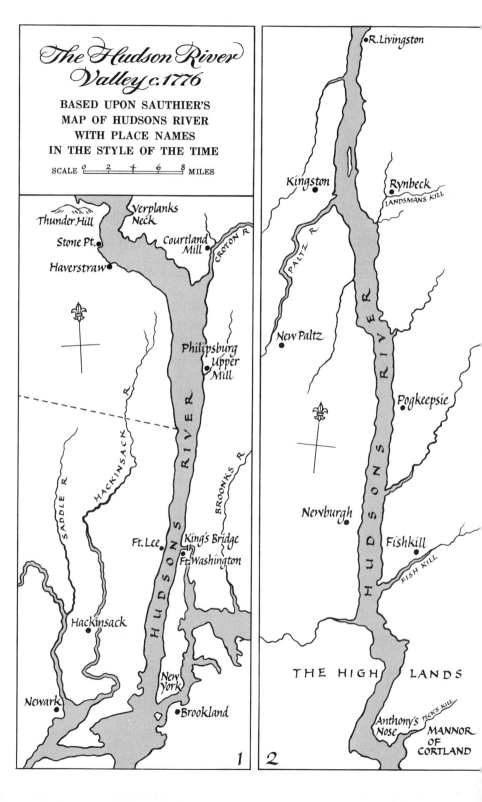

The Hudson River Valley c. 1776

BASED UPON SAUTHIER'S
MAP OF HUDSONS RIVER
WITH PLACE NAMES
IN THE STYLE OF THE TIME

SCALE 0 2 4 6 8 MILES

Thunder Hill

Verplanks Neck

Stone Pt.

Courtland Mill

CROTON R.

Haverstraw

Philipsburg Upper Mill

HACKINSACK R.

SADDLE R.

BROONKS R.

HUDSONS RIVER

Ft. Lee

King's Bridge

Ft. Washington

Hackinsack

New York

Newark

Brookland

1

R. Livingston

Kingston

Rynbeck

LANDSMANS KILL

PALTZ R.

New Paltz

Pogkeepsie

HUDSONS RIVER

Newburgh

Fishkill

FISH KILL

THE HIGH LANDS

Anthony's Nose

PECK'S KILL

MANNOR OF CORTLAND

2

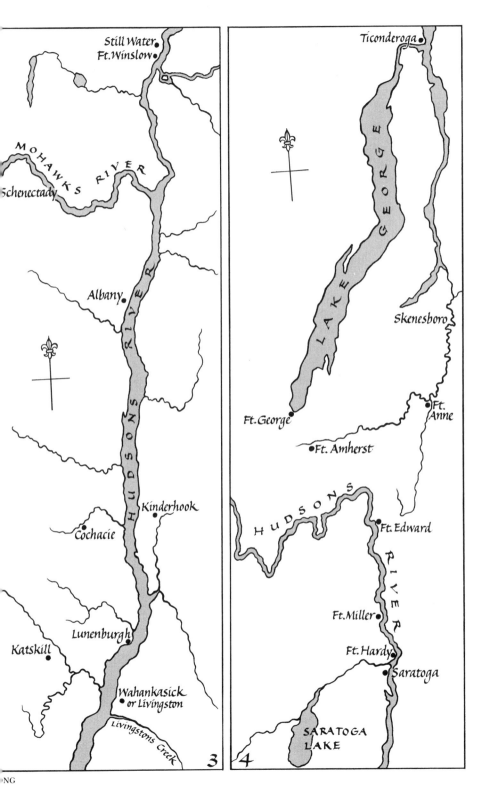

Still Water
Ft. Winslow

MOHAWKS RIVER

Schenectady

Albany

HUDSONS RIVER

Kinderhook

Cochacie

Lunenburgh

Katskill

Wahankasick
or Livingston

Livingstons Creek

3

Ticonderoga

LAKE GEORGE

Skenesboro

Ft. George

Ft. Anne

Ft. Amherst

HUDSONS RIVER

Ft. Edward

Ft. Miller

Ft. Hardy

Saratoga

SARATOGA LAKE

4

NG

PHILIP VAN CORTLANDT (1749–1831)

by Ezra Ames

The

Revolutionary War

Memoir

and

Selected Correspondence

of

Philip Van Cortlandt

Compiled and Edited
by
Jacob Judd

SLEEPY HOLLOW RESTORATIONS
Tarrytown, New York

First Printing

Copyright © 1976 by Sleepy Hollow Restorations, Inc.
All rights reserved.

For Information, address the publisher:
Sleepy Hollow Restorations, Inc.
Tarrytown, New York 10591

Library of Congress Cataloging in Publication Data
Main entry under title:
The Van Cortlandt family papers.
Includes bibliographical references and index.
1. Van Cortlandt family. I. Judd, Jacob, 1929–
CS71.V22175   1976   929'.2'0973   75-43652
ISBN 0-912882-27-1 (v. 1)

Van Cortlandt, Philip, 1749–1831.
The Revolutionary War memoir and selected correspondence
of Philip Van Cortlandt
(The Van Cortlandt family papers; v. 1)
Includes bibliographical references and index.
1. Van Cortlandt family. 2. Van Cortlandt, Philip, 1749–1831.
3. United States—History—Revolution, 1775–1783—Personal narratives.
I. Judd, Jacob, 1929-   II. Title.   III. Series.
CS71.V22175   1976   vol. 1   929'.2'0973s
ISBN 0-912882-27-1   [973.3'092'4] [B]   75-43654

DESIGNED BY RAY FREIMAN

Manufactured in the United States of America

Contents

CONTENTS

Maps & Illustrations

Preface

As part of its bicentennial activities in seeking to commemorate American independence, Sleepy Hollow Restorations, in conjunction with the New York State American Revolution Bicentennial Commission, has produced this Bicentennial edition of Philip Van Cortlandt's *Memoir* and Selected Correspondence. This edition serves as a prelude to a volume containing the complete correspondence spanning Philip's entire lifetime, and also stands on its own because of its Revolutionary War significance. The multi-volume publication of the Papers of the Van Cortlandt Family, now in progress, will contain the correspondence and business papers of Philip, his father, Pierre, Sr., and of his siblings, Pierre, Jr., Gilbert, Catharine, Cornelia, and Ann. Later volumes will contain the papers of earlier Van Cortlandts, commencing with the founder of the American branch, Oloff Stevense (Van Cortlandt).

The publication of this and the subsequent volumes of the Van Cortlandt Papers would not have been possible without the financial support of the New York State American Revolution Bicentennial Commission, the National Endowment for the Humanities, and Sleepy Hollow Restorations. Herbert H. Lehman College of the City

University of New York provided released time from teaching responsibilities so that this work could be completed.

Works of this nature cannot come to fruition without the aid of many libraries and librarians. Special thanks are due to the staffs of the Manuscript Divisions of the New York Public Library and of the New-York Historical Society. A full roster of institutions and libraries who deserve mention would necessarily include most of the major repositories across the country.

Research assistance was ably supplied by Don White of New York University and Stephen Schlesinger of Herbert H. Lehman College. I received invaluable suggestions from Mark D. Hirsch of Bronx Community College, CUNY, and from Barbara Chernow of the editorial staff of *The Papers of Alexander Hamilton*. The typing assignments were capably handled by Vivian Furgiuele, Lillian Hackbarth, and Karen Judd. Errors of omission and commission rest, of course, upon my shoulders.

Jacob Judd

Editorial Apparatus

THIS EDITOR BELONGS to the school of historians who believe that manuscript materials should be presented in a form as close as possible to the original. In that context, paragraphing, spelling, punctuation, and grammar have been followed as found in Philip Van Cortlandt's writings. Misspelled proper names have been corrected in the notes but not in the body of the manuscript materials. Similarly, superior letters and abbreviations have been retained, including the use of the ampersand (&). Only in those instances where the meaning may be unclear has additional information been included in brackets [ ]: for example, W.P. appears as W[hite] P [lains]. When Philip refers to Gen. W. it has not been deemed necessary to note that W. is, of course, Washington.

The punctuation of the original letters has been followed. This might create a comprehension problem at first, but upon reading a few pages of Philip's *Memoir* or correspondence, the natural pauses become more obvious. He followed a common practice of his time in using capital letters rather freely, but this should not pose a problem for the modern reader either.

Where material has been lost or destroyed, it will be so noted. Nothing has been arbitrarily deleted from this material. In a few instances, owing to Philip's handwriting, a word remains unclear. In those cases, an educated guess has been made and has been noted in brackets with an added question mark. The equivalent of typographical errors has been retained with corrections in brackets. Philip in one letter, for example, wrote "our Honoured Favour," when he obviously meant "Father," and his error has been so noted.

The annotations serve several purposes: to provide useful identifications for individuals and places, to supply background information, and to guide the reader to additional sources of information. They have purposely been kept concise, even though some of the subjects might easily have lent themselves to being treatises on outstanding events.

Abbreviations & Short Titles

&	And
&c	Etcetera
AD	Autograph Document
ADF	Autograph Draft
ADS	Autograph Document Signed
AL	Autograph Letter
ALS	Autograph Letter Signed
Df	Draft
Dfs	Draft Signed
LBC	Letter Book Copy
LC	Library of Congress
NYHS	The New-York Historical Society
NYPL	The New York Public Library
SHR	Sleepy Hollow Restorations

Alden	John R. Alden. *A History of the American Revolution* (New York, 1969).
Boatner	Mark M. Boatner, III. *Encyclopedia of the American Revolution* (New York, 1966 and 1974).
Cal. H. Mss.	Edmund B. O'Callaghan, ed. *Calendar of Historical Manuscripts Relating to the War of the Revolution in the Office of the Secretary of State* (Albany, 1868), 2 Vols.

Cook	Frederick Cook, ed. *Journals of the Military Expedition of Major General John Sullivan 1779* (Ann Arbor, Michigan, 1967, reprint of 1887 edition).
DAB	Dumas Malone, ed. *Dictionary of American Biography* (New York, 1922–1937), 22 Vols.
D. Col. N.Y.	Edmund B. O'Callaghan and Berthold Fernow, eds. *Documents Relative to the Colonial History of the State of New York* (Albany, 1856–1887), 15 Vols.
Fitzpatrick	John C. Fitzpatrick, ed. *The Writings of George Washington from the Original Manuscript Sources 1745–1799* (Washington, 1931–1944), 39 Vols.
Force, *Archives, IV*	Peter Force, ed. *American Archives: Fourth Series, Containing a Documentary History of the English Colonies in North America from the King's Message to Parliament of March 7, 1774, to the Declaration of Independence by the United States* (Washington, 1837–1846), 6 Vols.
Force, *Archives, V*	Peter Force, ed. *American Archives: Fifth Series, Containing a Documentary History from . . . July 4, 1776, to . . . September 3, 1783* (Washington, 1848–1853), 3 Vols.
French	J. H. French. *Gazetteer of the State of New York: Embracing a Comprehensive View of the Geography, Geology, and General History of the State . . .* (Syracuse, 1860).
Heitman	Francis B. Heitman. *Historical Register of Officers of the Continental Army During the War of the Revolution* (Reprint of 1914 edition, Baltimore, 1973).

N.Y. in Rev.	Berthold Fernow, ed. *New York in the Revolution* (Albany, 1887; reprinted 1972).
Papers of George Clinton	Hugh Hastings, ed. *Public Papers of George Clinton, First Governor of New York, 1777–1795, 1801–1804* (New York and Albany, 1899–1914), 10 Vols.
Roberts	James A. Roberts, comp. *New York in the Revolution* (Albany, 1901), 2 Vols.
Spafford	Horatio G. Spafford. *A Gazetteer of the State of New-York* (Albany, 1813).
Ward	Christopher Ward. *The War of the Revolution,* edited by John R. Alden (New York, 1952), 2 Vols.

Chronology *of*
Philip Van Cortlandt's Revolutionary
War Activities

1775
June 18: Commissioned as Lieutenant Colonel of Fourth New York Regiment.

August 26–28: Stationed at Albany.

November 5: Stationed at Fort Ticonderoga.

November: Recuperated from fever at General Philip Schuyler's home in Albany.

November: Received orders from General George Washington in New York City.

1776
May: Stationed at Albany.

June: Stationed at Fort Ticonderoga.

July 15: Sat on court-martial of Colonel Moses Hazen.

August 4: Visited James Van Cortlandt at Kingsbridge on day British landed at Throgs Neck.

August 7–23: Stationed at Skenesborough.

November 30: Appointed Colonel of Second New York Regiment.

December 2: Sat on court-martial of General Benedict Arnold.

Demember 24: Stationed in Bucks County, Pennsylvania.

1777
January: Stationed at General Washington's Headquarters in Morristown, New Jersey.

January 18: Stationed at Fishkill, New York. Commanded area from Morrisania to North River on mainland of New York north of Manhattan Island.

September-October: Stationed at Saratoga.

1778
January-June: Stationed at Valley Forge.

October-December: Participated in Western New York campaign.

1779
January-September: Engaged in Western New York campaign against the Indians.

October-December: His regiment constructed huts at Morristown, New Jersey.

1780
(December)-January: Sat on court-martial of General Benedict Arnold.

March 22-Spring: Stationed at General Washington's Headquarters in Morristown, New Jersey.

June-July: Stationed at West Point.

November-December: Stationed at Albany.

December: Appointed commanding officer of the combined Second and Fourth New York Regiments.

1781
January-August: Stationed at Albany and Fort Schuyler.

August: Prepared for aborted attack on New York City.

August 25-29: Marched through New Jersey.

September 15: Stationed at Baltimore.

October 13-17: Participated in Yorktown campaign.

October-November: Took charge of British prisoners following Yorktown campaign.

1782
April 29: Signed Army Officers' petition concerning arrears in pay; time of so-called "Newburgh Conspiracy."
May: Established last headquarters for New York forces at New Windsor.

1783
May: Became founding member of Society of the Cincinnati.

June: Presented colors and musical equipment of Second New York Regiment to General George Clinton, Governor of New York.

July-November: Waited for British evacuation of New York at family home in Croton.

September 30: Breveted a Brigadier General.

The

Revolutionary War

Memoir

and

Selected Correspondence

of

Philip Van Cortlandt

Biographical Sketch *of*
Philip Van Cortlandt

IT CAN TRULY BE SAID of Philip Van Cortlandt that he
was born with the proverbial "silver spoon in his mouth."
Heir to one of the great landed fortunes of New York, he
bore a name that exemplified political preeminence, social status, and economic well-being. Associated first with
the growth of New Netherland and later with that of New
York, the Van Cortlandts represented one of the
foremost families in the history of the province from the
1630s to the post-Revolutionary era. Philip should have
been able to look toward a life of relative affluence based
on his family properties, his surveying and business activities, and eventual office-holding. But this life of comfort was not to be; a time of turmoil intervened which
changed his existence from one of tranquility to that of a
battlefield commander.

Soldiering was not an alien activity to the Van
Cortlandts, for every generation in North America had
some representation in the military. This association
began with the founding of the North American branch
of the family by Oloff Stevense in 1638. A common
soldier in the employ of the West India Company, Oloff
soon added the patronymic "Van Cortlandt" to his name
and began a meteoric rise to a position of prominence in

3

the nascent colony. Starting his office-holding career as an inspector of tobacco in 1640, Oloff, some six years later, became a member of the short-lived legislative unit known as The Nine Men. Oloff filled many posts on the municipal and provincial levels between 1640 and his death in 1684. He did not forget his military past, because among his various capacities he served as a colonel in the Burghers' Corps, or municipal militia, helped improve the fortifications of Fort Amsterdam, and became a commissioner of Indian affairs for the province. While performing these duties, he acquired one of the great fortunes in the colony through his brewery activities.

The transfer of power from the Dutch to the English in the province did not seem to disturb him, for he continued to hold important offices under English rule and increased his business and land holdings.[1]

Oloff's eldest son, Stephanus (1643–1700), continued and expanded his father's achievements. His military services began with the rank of ensign in a Burgher Company and advanced to that of a captain. He was active in the campaign against the French and Indians in 1689, and finally achieved the title of colonel.

His civilian career covered judicial and legislative activities on the municipal and provincial levels. Stephanus' judicial career included service as first Judge of the Court of Admiralty, Judge of Superior Court of Pleas of Kings County, Associate Justice and later Chief Justice of the Supreme Court of the Province of New York, Justice of the Court of Oyer and Terminer (a special superior court), and Chancellor of the Court of Chancery.

On the legislative end, he served for years on the governor's council, a schepen under the Dutch and an alderman under the English. Receiver General of the

Province, in 1677 he achieved the distinction of becoming the first native-born Mayor of New York City. This did not end his career but merely whetted it, for he went on to become Commissioner of Customs and Collector of Revenue, and finally Secretary of the Province of New York.

Stephanus also maintained his father's brewery and carried forward the family activities in commerce. The status of the family was then augmented through his active acquisition of vast property holdings in the Province. Following the practice common in Europe for rising merchants to acquire land as a means to obtain elevated social prestige, Stephanus gathered together some eighty-six thousand acres in what is now Westchester County. Governor Benjamin Fletcher gave the land the status of a Manor in 1697, and granted Stephanus the title of Lord of the Manor.

Upon his death, the land descended to his heirs in roughly equal amounts. Stephanus thus followed the Dutch inheritance practices rather than adopting the English forms of entail and primogeniture. The land remained as a unit, however, until the death of his widow, Gertruyd Schuyler Van Cortlandt, in 1723. By 1734 the land divisions had been made and the title of Lord of the Manor was abandoned.

Probably the most controversial activity of Stephanus' long career concerned his role in the famous Leisler affair. As Secretary of the Province, Stephanus maintained the official records. Upon Jacob Leisler's assumption of control of the New York government following the collapse of King James' reign in 1688, Stephanus was ordered to surrender the records to the Leisler group. Van Cortlandt refused and the two became bitter enemies. With the return of the Province to established

5

Philip Van Cortlandt

Crown authority in 1691 under William and Mary, Stephanus sat on the Council which decreed in May of that year that Leisler should be executed for his treasonable activities. Subsequently, the Leislers were successful in achieving a royal pardon and apology for the humiliation and execution of their kin.[2]

Stephanus' eldest son, John or Johannes (1672–1702), held a commission as ensign in the New York City Regiment. On John's death, his land passed to his brother, Oliver (1678–1708), who soon died. As a result, the third brother, Philip (1683–1748), our subject's grandfather, inherited his father's share of the estate.

Philip followed the family pattern of involvement in governmental activities. He served as an alderman and member of the governor's council. Extremely active as a merchant, he acquired additional city property, including a coffee house and a tavern, The Fighting Cocks.

Of Philip's five sons, the one most important to our story is Pierre (1721–1814), youngest brother among the siblings. Pierre inherited the Manor House in Croton-on-Hudson, and he was, of course, the father of Philip. Pierre held a commission as colonel of the Westchester Militia and quite possibly saw action in the last of the French and Indian Wars.

Of more importance were Pierre's political activities. The elected representative to the New York General Assembly from Van Cortlandt Manor in 1768, he became Lieutenant Governor of the State of New York in 1777, a position he held until his political retirement in 1795. A man who was not given to speechmaking, he apparently had extraordinary administrative abilities which were recognized by his peers. As a result, Pierre served in several of the Provincial Congresses, became a member of and later president of the influential Com-

6

mittee of Safety, and then Lieutenant Governor. With the elected Governor, George Clinton, serving in the Continental Army as a field officer, the administering of the revolutionary government fell upon the capable Pierre. His contribution to the revolutionary cause was rewarded by the electorate who repeatedly chose him for the second spot in the state administration.

The warmth of his fatherly concern for Philip is easily discerned in the selected letters included in the Correspondence in this volume. His administrative tasks and the war upheavals kept him removed from his home on the Croton River until shortly before his death. But in the intervening years he paid close attention to the details necessary in maintaining and supervising the remaining Van Cortlandt properties in the Manor. (A full biographical sketch of Pierre will appear in a subsequent volume in this series.) Apparently his gift for detail and his administrative abilities were passed down to his sons, Philip and Pierre, Jr.

Philip thus inherited a long family tradition of service, both governmental and military. According to his *Memoir*, by the time he was twenty-five years of age he had become a major in the Westchester Militia and, shortly thereafter, would rise in rank to that of lieutenant colonel and later colonel in the American Revolutionary forces. As his military career is amply covered by the *Memoir* and his Selected Correspondence, we will here primarily concern ourselves with his governmental activities.

The importance of the Van Cortlandts' connection with the revolutionary movement in New York is exemplified by their association with the various Provincial Congresses. The General Assembly of New York, that is, the royally authorized legislative body, passed out of

7

Philip Van Cortlandt

existence in April 1775 and was replaced by a series of *ad hoc* revolutionary provincial legislative groups, prior to the establishment of a constitutional New York State government. Either Philip or his father served in each of the four Provincial Congresses; Philip in the First, and Pierre in the others. The major actions of the First Provincial Congress consisted of appointing representatives to the Second Continental Congress and raising an armed force in New York. For the latter purpose, Philip was given his commission as lieutenant colonel. Philip rapidly ceased being an elected representative and began a military career which lasted until the final ousting of the British from New York in November 1783.

There are some aspects of Philip's military career, only briefly mentioned in the *Memoir* or his Selected Correspondence, which are worthy of further attention. They are his constant concern with the rate of pay, the slowness in payment by the Continental Congress, the difficulty in acquiring arms and supplies from the New York administration, and the struggle for recognition of his rank in relation to other officers appointed at a later time or originally appointed at a lower grade. The comprehensive volume of his correspondence will present many examples of these concerns throughout the war years.

Although he may originally have been granted his high rank because of his family's status and his father's position in the revolutionary movement, Philip constantly emphasized that he wished the state and the appropriate members of the Continental Congress to consider him on the basis of his achievements and his steadfast loyalty despite many bitter personal sacrifices. To some extent, he was rewarded by being promoted to colonel and given command of his own regiment. The

8

monetary and supply problems would continue to plague him along with many other officers up to the final army encampment at New Windsor.

Philip was fortunate in that he survived the war in reasonably good health, with the exception of the fever and ague that troubled him during his first year in service. The various epidemics, particularly smallpox, did not affect him. He does not mention whether he had been infected as a child, or whether he had been inoculated at some time, but in either case he was apparently immune to that extremely dangerous disease.

At the conclusion of the conflict, he returned to the family home at Croton and made it his main residence for the remainder of his life. Both opposing sides had spared the home from the torch, and with only minor repairs necessary the Manor House could again soon become serviceable. The homes of the major figures on both sides of the conflict were left relatively unscathed in what seems to have been an unwritten agreement among the military forces.

Philip did not have much time to relax. He was appointed by Governor Clinton as a Commissioner of Forfeiture for the Southern District. Under several acts of the State Legislature in the 1770s the real and personal property belonging to New Yorkers attainted of loyalty to the Crown were to be seized and subject to later sale. The personal properties were then sold by the Commissioners of Sequestration while the real properties were handled by the Commissioners of Forfeiture. Philip's associate for the Southern District was Isaac Stoutenburgh. The District included Westchester, Kings, New York, Queens, Richmond, and Suffolk counties. Among the attainted Loyalists in the District were two of the wealthiest families of New York, the Philipses and the

9

DeLanceys. So it is no wonder to learn that the two commissioners had the largest amount of sales in the state, amounting to some £502,709.[3]

He faithfully performed the task and transmitted his accounts to the appropriate governmental agencies. The only criticism of his role as commissioner came during the hotly contested election of 1808, when Philip was accused of having speculated in state certificates in the process of selling the former Loyalist estates. The anonymous accuser asserted that, "Gen. Van Cortlandt, more attentive to his *private interest*, than to his *public duties*, and believing that the price of certificates would be greatly reduced, as soon as the sales of the forfeited estates should be closed, he determined to accumulate a fortune at the expense of the public. . . ."[4] The writer was suggesting that Philip had obtained depreciated certificates in the process of the land sales and subsequently sold these certificates at a discount in the hope that the value of the certificates would further depreciate so he could buy them back for less than he had originally received. The plan went awry, declared the writer, because Alexander Hamilton's funding schemes raised the value of certificates instead of reducing them. Since no other action was taken to follow this charge, it can be assumed that it was part of an election campaign effort aimed at defeating the Jeffersonian Republicans, a party in which Philip was prominent.

No sooner had Philip concluded his activities as commissioner in 1788 than he was chosen as a representative from Westchester County to the Constitutional Convention which met in Poughkeepsie in June 1788 to determine whether New York should adopt the proposed Constitution of the United States. The contest over this issue was a hotly debated one with such leading strong central government advocates as Alexander Hamilton and John Jay arguing the case for adoption. Their newspaper articles later came to be known as *The Federalist Papers*. Leading the opposition was Governor George Clinton with support from his Lieutenant Governor, Pierre Van Cortlandt. This question over ratification sharply divided the State, and New York was the eleventh state to ratify the Constitution. Many agreed with Clinton's and Abraham Yates' carefully reasoned declarations that in due time the states would lose most of their sovereign powers to the newly created central government. It was into this political maelstrom that Philip was thrust.

After much debate, which lasted most of the summer, a majority agreed to accept the Constitution, on the condition, however, that amendments would be adopted shortly to guarantee individual rights. Philip split away from Clinton and his father to vote for ratification.[5] This must have been an extremely important political step for him to take in view of his father's role in the state government.

Philip's position was the popular one in Westchester and within a few months he was elected a member of the State Assembly. Six days after taking his seat in that body, he found his name among six submitted for nomination as Congressmen by the supporters of the Constitution. His name was withdrawn when it was decided that only five men would be selected. It did not make much difference, for the so-called Antifederalists successfully elected their entire slate.

Philip was reelected to the Assembly in 1789 and, upon completion of that annual term, was elected to the State Senate, where he served for three terms.

His highest political position was reached in 1793,

when he became a member of the House of Representatives in the Third Congress. Almost immediately upon being seated, Philip was assigned to various committees which dealt with militarily related matters. His first important committee assignment came in February 1794, when he was placed on the politically sensitive committee to investigate the "state of the Treasury Department." It was politically sensitive because Congress sought to assert its prerogatives over control of the Federal finances, in a spirit of rebellion against Alexander Hamilton's one-man rule of the Treasury.

Elected to the House as a Federalist supporter, Philip along with other representatives from landed districts in New York and Virginia soon joined the opposition group headed by Thomas Jefferson and James Madison. Philip supported measures to improve the militia forces in the states in light of the British and Indian threat in the upper Ohio Territory, first voted against and later for an expansion of the Navy, and opposed President Washington's assertion that the Whisky Rebellion was a manifestation of rising discontent fomented by "self-created societies."

When Washington retired from office at the end of his second term, the Jeffersonian Republicans attempted to insert a paragraph into the House's response to Washington's address to them in order to be on record as favoring his voluntary retirement, because it would establish a precedent: "For our country's sake, for the sake of republican liberty, it is our earnest wish that your example may be the guide of your successors; and thus, after being the ornament and safeguard of the present age, become the patrimony of our descendants." But this was too much for Philip, and he voted against the proposal.

During John Adams' administration, Philip was staunchly aligned with the opposition. It is to his credit that he voted to uphold Matthew Lyon's right to retain his seat in Congress, although he was being prosecuted by the federal government under the terms of the Sedition Law for having published libelous statements against President Adams.

It was Philip's pleasure to be a member of the House which decided upon the choice of the third President. Soon after casting his vote in the New York delegation for Jefferson, he asked for and received leave to absent himself from the House for the remainder of the session.

Philip returned to Congress on December 7, 1801, for the Seventh Congress, which met for the first time in the District of Columbia, the nation's new capital. As in previous sessions Philip was placed on committees concerned with military affairs. In this first Congress of Jefferson's administration he supported the major Republican measures, but balked on occasion. He supported the repeal of Hamilton's internal taxes, the repeal of the Naturalization Act, and the passage of amendments to the Constitution so as to change the presidential and vice-presidential election procedures, but he sought to maintain Congressional control over changes in the governmental structures in the territories and supported a Congressional voice in decisions over the Louisiana Territory. He, of course, soon voted to uphold Jefferson's purchase of that disputed territory, but at the same time he wanted more of the diplomatic papers made available to Congress. Jefferson's second administration is noted for his belligerent attitude toward Great Britain as a result of the Napoleonic difficulties. In order to strengthen his hand, Jefferson, who had at first opposed an increased Navy, now sought to acquire one rapidly.

Philip Van Cortlandt

As an Army officer, Philip saw little use for naval armaments. Although he voted for a money appropriation so that Jefferson could build his famous fleet of fifty gunboats, when the President sought additional funds for six warships in March 1806, Philip voted in the negative. Just a year later, Philip had a change of heart and led the group seeking additional funds for gunboats and "other armed vessels." Perhaps his New York merchant friends and relatives had convinced him of the necessity for an expanded Navy.

Throughout his Congressional career, Philip voted for measures which would improve the lot of the Continental veterans, and usually supported claims of former officers for additional compensation. His attitude toward social change was more ambivalent. While in favor of George Rapp's purchase of lands for a new communal settlement of the Society of New Harmony, he voted against the resolution that, "from and after the 4th of July, 1805, all blacks and 'People of color' that shall be born within the District of Columbia, or whose mother shall be the property of any person residing within the district shall be free." While he and his father both owned slaves at the time, he subsequently did support a measure to curb the further importation of slaves into the nation.

Even Congressmen have lighter moments, and one came for Philip in January 1803 when a fellow Westchesterite, Daniel Lewis, petitioned the government for adequate compensation for his discovery of a medicine "which, in no case in which has been administered has failed of curing the bite of a mad dog. . . ." Philip reported to the House later that month that it was his committee's opinion "That the prayer of the said memorial ought not to be granted."

As the maritime differences with Great Britain and France grew more serious in the later months of 1808, Philip sided with the minority who did not join in the move toward a total embargo. With James Madison waiting to assume the presidency after the election of 1808, the "lame-duck" session of the Tenth Congress moved to repeal the Embargo Act. Whether it was because he realized that his career in the House was at an end, or whether he felt so strongly about this issue, Philip became a floor leader for the first time in the House in the move to repeal the embargo. He must have felt highly gratified when the House voted 81 to 40 in favor of lifting the embargo.[6]

Philip cast his last vote at five o'clock in the afternoon of March 3, 1809, and brought his political career to a close. His retirement came at the age of sixty, when most assumed that threescore and ten was beyond attainment.

For Philip, political retirement meant that he could return to his home at Croton and superintend the orchards and mills thriving on his lands. He kept in contact with Washington affairs through his brother Pierre, who served in the Eleventh and Twelfth Congresses, and through his assiduous newspaper reading. Politics again intervened in 1812 in the midst of the important presidential election. Madison sought reelection but was challenged by the New Yorker, DeWitt Clinton. Closely associated with the Clintons through the revolutionary cause, in politics, and by marriage, it is no surprise to learn that Philip voted for Clinton.[7]

He remained a bachelor, but he had the companionship of his sister Catharine, who was widowed in 1786. Philip invited Catharine and her children to reside with him at the Manor House, and he regarded her children with great affection. This was manifest in Philip's deci-

15

sion to grant residence privileges to his nephew, Pierre C. Van Wyck.

His retirement was broken in 1824 when General LaFayette traveled from France to make a triumphal tour of America. Philip graciously accepted the opportunity to meet with and accompany his old comrade-in-arms on part of his journey through New York. Perhaps it was this reliving of the glories of the past that induced Philip to transmit his war recollections to paper shortly thereafter.

He continued to live quietly at his country estate until the old soldier died on November 5, 1831. He is buried in the Van Cortlandtville cemetery in Peekskill, New York in sight of a home occupied by his parents for several years after the Revolution.

NOTES

1. Biographical accounts of the early Van Cortlandts can be found in *DAB*, Vol. XIX; L. Effingham DeForest, *The Van Cortlandt Family* (New York, 1930); Martha Lamb, "The Van-Cortlandt Manor-House," *Magazine of American History*, Vol. XV. No. 3 (March, 1886), 209–236; Catherine E. Van Cortlandt, "The Van Cortlandt Family," in J. T. Scharf, ed., *History of Westchester County, New York* . . . (Philadelphia, 1886), II, 423–436.

2. For a discussion of this turbulent period of New York history see, Michael H. Hall, Lawrence H. Leder, and Michael Kammen, eds., *Glorious Revolution in America: Documents on the Colonial Crisis of 1689* (New York, 1964); and David Lovejoy, *The Glorious Revolution in America* (New York, 1972).

3. Roberts, II, 260–261.

4. [Anon.], "To The Electors Of The County of Westchester," Broadside [1808], NYPL Mss. Div.

5. A thorough study of the Convention and the ensuing debate can be found in Linda Grant DePauw, *The Eleventh Pillar: New York State and the Federal Constitution* (Ithaca, N.Y., 1966); the official record of the Convention appears in: New York State, *Debates and Proceedings of the Convention of the State of New-York* (New York, 1788).

6. The analysis of Philip's career in Congress is based on the *Journals of the House of Representatives of the United States* for the Third, Fourth, Fifth, Sixth, Seventh, Eighth, Ninth, and Tenth Congresses, published in 1826.

7. Marshall Smelser, *The Democratic Republic, 1801–1815* (New York, 1968), pp. 247–248; Jabez D. Hammond, *The History of Political Parties in the State of New York, From the Ratification of the Federal Constitution to December, 1840* (Cooperstown, New York, 1844), I, 321–322.

Genealogy *of* Philip Van Cortlandt's Branch *of the Family*

OLOFF STEVENSE VAN CORTLANDT   Founder of New World branch of family.
  b. In Holland ca. 1600–1610. Arrived in New Netherland in 1638.
  m. Annetje Loockermans in New Amsterdam.
  d. 1684.

CHILDREN OF OLOFF AND ANNETJE (LOOCKERMANS) VAN CORTLANDT

1. STEPHANUS
          First native-born Mayor of New York, 1677.
   b. May 7, 1643.
   m. Gertruyd Schuyler of Albany, September 10, 1671.
   d. November 25, 1700.
2. Maria
   b. 1645.
   m. Jeremias Van Rensselaer,
          Fourth Patroon of Rensselaerswyck, April 27, 1662.
   d. 1689.
3. Johannes
   b. October 11, 1648.
   d. 1667.
4. Sophia
   b. May 31, 1651.
   m. Andries Teller, May 6, 1671.
   d. Will dated September 20, 1728; will proved October 1, 1729.

Philip Van Cortlandt

5. Catherine
    b. October 25, 1652.
    m. (1) John Dervall, October 10, 1675.
        d. Will proved March 5, 1689.
    (2) Frederick Philipse, 1692.
        d. Will dated January 7, 1730.
6. Cornelia
    b. November 21, 1655.
    m. Brandt Schuyler, July 12, 1682.
    d. February 18, 1689.
7. Jacobus
        Founder of the branch of the family which settled on land
        now known as Van Cortlandt Park.
    b. July 7, 1658.
    m. Eva (DeVries) Philipse, May 31, 1691.
    d. 1739.

CHILDREN OF STEPHANUS AND GERTRUDE
(SCHUYLER) VAN CORTLANDT

1. Johannes
    b. October 24, 1672.
    m. Anna Sophia Van Schaick, 1695.
    d. ———.
2. Margaret
    b. July 2, 1674.
    m. (1) Samuel Bayard, March 12, 1696.
        d. Will proved January 30, 1746.
    (2) Peter Kemble.
    d. ———.
3. Ann
    b. February 13, 1676.
    m. Stephen DeLancey, January 23, 1700.
    d. ———.
4. Oliver
    b. October 26, 1678.
    d. 1708.

5. Maria
   b. April 4, 1680.
   m. (1) Kiliaen Van Rensselaer, October 15, 1701.
         d. 1719.
      (2) John Miln.
   d. ———.
6. Gertrude
   b. January 1681.
   d. ———.
7. PHILIP
   b. August 9, 1683.
   m. Catharine DePeyster.
   d. September 2, 1748.
8. Stephan
   b. August 11, 1685 [1695?].
   m. Catalina Staats, August 28, 1713.
   d. 1756.
9. Gertrude
   b. October 1688.
   m. Col. Henry Beekman, 1726.
   d. March 23, 1777.
10. Gysbert
    Bapt. October 7, 1689.
    d. ———.
11. Elizabeth
    b. 1691.
    d. young.
12. Elizabeth
    b. May 24, 1694.
    m. Rev. William Skinner.
    d. ———.
13. Catharine
    b. June 24, 1696.
    m. Andrew Johnston.
    d. ———.

Philip Van Cortlandt

14. Cornelia
    b. July 30, 1698.
    m. Col. John Schuyler, October 18, 1723.
    d. ca. 1777.

CHILDREN OF PHILIP AND CATHARINE (DePEYSTER) VAN CORTLANDT

1. Stephen
   b. October 26, 1711.
   m. Mary W. Ricketts, May 6, 1738.
   d. October 17, 1756.

2. Abraham
   b. October 19, 1713.
   d. 1746.

3. Philip
   b. February 29, 1715.
   d. 1745.

4. John
   b. September 9, 1718.
   d. 1747.

5. PIERRE
   b. January 21, 1721.
   m. Joanna Livingston, May 28, 1748.
   d. May 1, 1814.

6. Catharine
   b. June 26, 1725.
   d. June 4, 1735.

CHILDREN OF PIERRE AND JOANNA (LIVINGSTON) VAN CORTLANDT

1. PHILIP
   b. August 21, 1749.
   d. November 5, 1831.

2. Catharine
   b. July 4, 1751.
   m. Abraham Van Wyck, September 21, 1748.
      d. January 1786.
   d. September 29, 1829.

3. Cornelia
   b. August 2, 1753.
   m. Gerard G. Beekman, Jr., 1769.
      d. 1822.
   d. March 14, 1847.

4. Gertrude
   b. June 26, 1755.
   d. December 9, 1766.

5. Gilbert
   b. April 6, 1757.
   d. November 12, 1786.

6. Stephen
   b. February 13, 1760.
   d. August 29, 1775.

7. Pierre
   b. August 29, 1762.
   m. (1) Catherine (Clinton) Taylor.
         d. January 10, 1811.
      (2) Ann Stevenson, May 10, 1813.
         d. February 20, 1821.
   d. June 13, 1848.

8. Ann
   b. June 1, 1766.
   m. Philip S. Van Rensselaer.
      d. September 25, 1824.
   d. January 10, 1855.

CHILDREN OF ABRAHAM AND CATHARINE
(VAN CORTLANDT) VAN WYCK

1. Theodorus Cortlandt
   b. ———.
   m. Mary Howell Stretch, 1800.
   d. 1840.
2. Pierre Cortlandt
   b. ———.
   d. Prior to 1829.
3. Philip Gilbert
   b. 1786.
   m. Mary Gardiner.
   d. 1870.

CHILDREN OF PIERRE AND ANN (STEVENSON)
VAN CORTLANDT

1. Pierre
   b. April 25, 1815.
   m. Catharine Elizabeth Beck, June 14, 1836.
   d. July 11, 1884.

Introduction *to*
the Memoir

PHILIP VAN CORTLANDT used his own Revolutionary War notes, diary entries, and correspondence, all of which had been kept in pristine condition by the family, to prepare the interesting autobiographical account of his wartime activities herein referred to as his *Memoir*. There is no question that it was written shortly after 1824, when Philip was more than seventy-six years old, and some forty-two years after the conclusion of the Revolution. The evidence for the approximate date of writing the *Memoir* appears in his opening genealogical remarks, wherein he refers to the death of his brother-in-law, Philip S. Van Rensselaer, which had occurred in 1824, and notes that the widow continued to live in their Albany residence. This places the writing of the *Memoir* no earlier than 1825; it was concluded some time prior to his death in 1831.

Whether he ever intended to continue the story of his activities into the post-Revolutionary era when he became a New York Commissioner of Forfeiture, a member of the State Legislature, and then a representative in Congress is a moot issue. The abruptness of the concluding statements could have been the result of age debilities, a lack of a desire to continue into his postwar political career, or his impending death. Regardless of motives, the detailed account of his war career remains a superb contemporary document.

If these had been simply the reminiscences of a septuagenarian attempting to recapture the most dramatic years of his life, they could be questioned on several historical grounds. However, there is ample documentation for almost every statement, as a result of the Van Cortlandt family's sense of history and their efforts at preserving documents. Philip could also draw on the related correspondence of his father, Pierre Van Cortlandt, who served during the war as a presiding officer of the New York Committee of Safety and as Lieutenant Governor of New York. It was not necessary, therefore, for him to rely exclusively on memory, for he could turn to manuscript sources which were readily at hand.

Why did he write the *Memoir*? This is a question not easily answered. It might have been at the suggestion of various members of the family or possibly it was intended as his contribution to a more comprehensive work about the Revolution which was never written.

As for the *Memoir* itself, Philip aptly states that he was taught to "write badly" and his struggle with convoluted sentences is soon apparent to the reader. He had no concern for punctuation, grammatical niceties, or consistency in spelling. There is the strong possibility that the entire *Memoir* was prepared in draft form with the intention of having some other hand organize it for publication. The *Memoir* remained in the family possession for an additional forty-seven years after Philip's death before it appeared in print in 1878 in the pages of the *Magazine of American History*. It was published in a heavily edited version prepared by Dr. Pierre C. Van Wyck, Philip's grandnephew through his sister Catharine. Pierre Van Wyck added innumerable punctuation marks, modified the spelling, rearranged the material into paragraphs, and on occasion altered the sentence structure of the original to suit his own tastes. Some major variations between the two versions will be cited where appropriate in the notes.

The version published here is in the original form, complete with its glaring grammatical, spelling, and composition errors. It retains the vivid sound and cadence of Philip Van Cortlandt's own writing and speech patterns. He provides a portrayal of his activities in which he never really paints himself as the hero of any of the battles. Only once does he seem to step out of character by declaring that it was his effective warning which saved Albany from an attack by Burgoyne's forces. An analysis of the available materials relating to the events surrounding the campaign does not bear out Philip's contention. However, it is obvious that he believed in the importance of his warning up to the time of his death. (See *Memoir* pp. 46–47).

What emerges from the *Memoir* is a portrait of a dedicated field commander who knew how to carry out orders effectively. He cared for his men, and tried to obtain all that he could for their comfort. Well regarded by those he commanded and in turn by his superior

27

officers, Philip established a reputation as a reliable, efficient, and likable officer. Because he was present at many of the important events of the Revolutionary War, his account helps to enhance our knowledge and at the same time provides us with a further opportunity to commiserate with those officers and men of the New York regiments who struggled so long and valiantly to achieve an independent nation. It was a rare occasion, indeed, when Philip and his men could find a reason or the time to celebrate.

THE ATLANTIC SEABOARD

Philip Van Cortlandt saw action in an area extending from northern New York to southern Virginia. The magnitude of the territory covered by his troops can best be understood by following their peripatetic movements on the map (page 29).

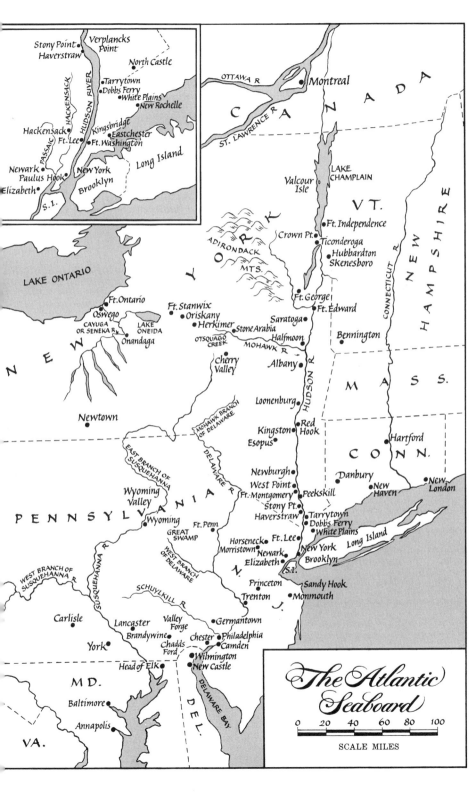

The Atlantic Seaboard

SCALE MILES

0   20   40   60   80   100

Memoir

This is to certify to all whom it may concern
that Gen[l]. Philip Van Cortlandt of the Town of Cortlandt, in the County of Westchester and State of New
York, eldest son of Pierre Van Cortlandt and Joanna
Livingston his wife was born in the City of New York in
a house in Stone Street near the Fort, on the 21st day
of August, old stile 1749, which makes his anniversary
Birthday the 1st day of September new stile.[1]

Shortly after the Decease of his Grand Father the
Honorable Philip Van Cortlandt he was born and his
Father and Mother removed to their Manor of Cortlandt
and possessed the House and lot at Croton, the House
having been built and together with the lot of land given
in tale to the said Pierre Van Cortlandt during his life
then to his eldest son. The above is as related to the son by
the Father, and Mother, who now certifies of his own
knowledge and memory as follows:———I remember
Three Sisters, Catharine, Cornelia and Gertruyd, the last
died when about eleven years old. I remember Three
Brothers, Gilbert, Stephen and Pierre, Stephen Died in
the year 1775, after I left him at Croton when I went as

Philip Van Cortlandt

Lieut. Colo. in the Revolutionary army. The youngest
Sister Ann was born at Croton, where all my Brothers
and Sisters were born. My sister Catherine was married
to Abraham Van Wyck son of Theodorus Van Wyck of
New York and has three sons the youngest Philip G. Van
Wyck was born after the death of his father. Sister Cor-
nelia married Gerard G. Beekman, Junr. son of Gerard
G. Beekman of New York and has had three Sons and
one Daughter Gerard, Pierre Cortlandt, Ann and
Stephen. Pierre Cortlandt was a very fine, good young
man he Died in the West Indies. Her husband died at the
Mills where she now resides. Sister Ann married Philip S.
Van Renselaer, who was a long time Mayor of Albany, he
Died in the year 1824 at his house in Albany where my
sister now resides. My brother Gilbert Died in New York
in the 29 year of his age of a white swelling which by
Emproper treatment thro the ignorance of a doctor
brought on a mortification of which he died———a truly
patient and Penitent man. My brother Pierre married
Catherine Clinton who died without issue. he then married Ann Stevenson who Died after leaving a son Pierre
who is a fine youth and I hope will live and become a fine
and worthy man.[2]

In my youthfull days my father had a small school-
house built on this farm about half a mile from the house
where I was taught in company with my sisters &
brothers and a few children of the neighbours by a
Common Schoolmaster, to read, write badly and something of arithmatick untill the age of fifteen when I was
sent to Coldenham Academy under the tuition of a
young Scotchman who Cadwalader Colden had

employed to conduct the school. His name was William Addams, who afterwards became a doctor, and Died in Mount Pleasant. I remained with Adams about Nine Months and applied closely to my studies and learnt arithmatick, surveying, mensuration, Book-keeping, dialling, gauging & logarithms, &c., &c.[3] On hearing of the death of my uncle and friend Captain Samuel Livingston my mothers brother who was drownded at sea, I left the academy and was frequently ingaged with Nathaniel Merritt a Surveyor who was mostly in the employ of my Father and his friends. Untill I became a Practical Surveyor myself and was frequently employed by Heirs of my great grandfather Stephanus Van Cortlandt surveying and disposing of lands in the Manor of Cortlandt. I was also engaged in the Milling business by the assistance and approbation of my father and also in keeping a small retail store. During this period my Father was a member of the Legislature and one of the number opposed to the odious Incroachments of the Crown and when every art and address was made use of to seduce members to join their party.[4] I remember Governor Tryon came on a visit bringing his Wife and a young Lady, who was a Daughter of the Honorable John Watts a relation of my fathers and Colo. Edmund Fanning his friend and Secretary[5] and after remaining a Night he proposed a Walk and after proceeding to the highest point of land on the farm being a height which affords a most delightfull prospect. When the Governor commenced with observing what great favours could be obtained if my father would relinquish his opposition to the views of the King and Parliament of Great Brittain

33

Philip Van Cortlandt

what grants of Land could and would be the consequence
in addition to other favours of Emmense consequence,
&c., &c. My Father then observed that he was chosen a
representative by unanimous approbation of a people
who placed a confidence in his integraty to use all his
ability for their benefit and the good of his country as a
true patriot which line of conduct he was determined to
pursue. The Governor then turned to Colo. Fanning and
said I find our business here must terminate for nothing
can be effected in this place so we will return. Which they
did by taking a short and hasty farewell & embarked on
board the sloop and returned to N York. this was in the
year 1774.[6] Previous to this Governor Tryon Introduced
the raising of Companies of Militia and granting com-
missions to officers as Tryon's Guards. And among them
sent me a commission as Major and as such I did exercise
the Reg[t]. in the Manor of Cortlandt of which James Ver
Planck was Colonel.[7] I was also frequently taken by my
Tory Relations to dine at the Fort with the Governor and
at other times with their own families. hoping perhaps to
prejudice me in their favour. but they were deceived For
in the Spring of the Year 1775 observing that a crisis was
fast approaching when it would be necessary to take an
active position either for or against our Country I did not
hesitate, but Immediately declarid my intention of risqu-
ing my all my property and life if necessary in the Defence of my Country. I did so and was Elected in the
County of Westchester in which I lived a Member of the
State Convention. The Battle at Lexington and Concord
having taken place and Eathan Allen having taken
Ticonderoga and Congress having determined to send

34

Troops to Canada I was solicited to take a Command as
Lieut. Colo. under James Holmes in the 4th Battalion of
New York Troops to be commissioned by John Hancock
President of Congress and Rich^d. Montgomery to be the
General in command. My assent was no longer witheld
than to obtain the full approbation of my Parents which
was immediately complyed with and I received the
Commission dated the 18th of June, 1775, and was order
on command without loss of time to Albany there to
dicipline equip and forward on the Troops, having left at
my departure my two Brothers Gilbert and Stephen at
the point of death with the malignant sore throat. One of
which I never saw afterwards as Stephen died a few days
after my departure in his 15th year. thus I left my friends
and all my property among which was a store of goods
and debts due me from an abandoned set of Tories,
almost all of which became a total loss. My anxiety and
trialls were from the time I received the Commission
many considering my youth and inexperiance the first
was at Newtown on Long Island where I mustered a
Company under the command of Capt. Abm. Riker the
Men had Inlisted under a promise of clothing, &c. and
requested of me if they could depend on having them
when upon hearing the negative they all walked off said
they were sorry but could not continue whereupon I gave
them my promise that I would furnish them out of my
own purse on which they returned with cheers of
applause. My next business was to inform the Convention in New York what I had promised which produced
the desired resolution that not only that Company, but all
the Troops should be provided with clothing, &c. as I

Philip Van Cortlandt

had proscribed for them. My next troubles was in Albany for on the arrival of Recruits without Arms or Tents I had first to Detain the sloops that brought them or hire Houses to accomodate them all which I had to advance pay for at a high price, and to keep them with me to advance my own money and borrow of a friend sufficient to pay one Dollar Each to upwards 350 soldiers. At length I took possession of what I found out to be the Kings Store which I made use of as a Barrack for the men but Want of more cash at length produced a serious mutiny and at the time when I received the disagreeable tidings of my Brothers decease. Having perused the letter giving the information I dismissed the parade consisting of about 400 Men as yet without arms, and retired to my Room grieving for the Loss of my favorite Brother. In about one hour two of my officers came and Informed me that 181 of the Men had gone off and that all the Rest was preparing to follow them unless I could prevent them. I took my Sword in my hand and went with them to the Barracks where I found the Men in great disorder, but passing that all might see me without speaking to any of them, untill I had resolved how to conduct so as first to allarm then to soothe their passions in my favour if possible I therefore Injoined it on the two officers to prevent by seizing my hands any Injury to be done to any one with my sword, which I am happy to say was affected and all in a few minutes became my friends and volunteers brought back the Deserters who was pardoned by and with consent of Colo. Van Schaack[8] who fortunately arrived to my assistance. All the troops having passed I followed altho unwell to Ticonderoga where I was

confined with a fever and for some time at the point of
Death and in my convalessant state Genl. Schuyler
brought me to his House in Albany after which he permitted me to return and Visit my friends during the
remaining part of the Winter and untill I should receive
further orders. during this period my Colo. James
Holmes left our servis and Colo. Jacobus Wynkoop was
appointed to take the command of the 4th Reg^t. and
Early in the spring of 1776, ordered to command at
Ticonderoga Not hearing from Genl. Schuyler I went to
New York and waiting on the Commander in Chief General Washington who Expected the British Army from
Boston Intended to attack the City of New York give me
orders to go to Genl. Schuyler where I should be directed
how the Regiment should be disposed off Either to the
north or to join the grand Army under his command the
result was Genl. Schuyler sent me to my Reg^t. at Ticonderoga when our army Retreated from Canada.[9] General Gates arrived and comm^d at Ticonderoga and Colo.
Wynkoop sent to Schenesborough. myself being ordered
on a Court Martial Continued for the Trial of Colo.
Moses Hazen arrested by Genl. Arnold of Disobediance
of Orders. I remained time sufficient to discover the Vile
Conduct of Arnold in procuring a Vast Quantity of
goods from the Merchants of Montrial which he intended and which I believe was appropriated to his benefit and also for improper conduct before the Court he
would have been arrested himself but escaped by procuring an order from Genl. Gates to send me the morning
after the Court had adjourned to Schenesborough, by
which means the Court was Desolved, Hazen released

from arrest, & Arnold escaped Sensure which he ought to have had.[10]

On my arrival at Scheensboro I found my Colo. Winkoop very unwell and he directed me to take the Command and forward on the troops arriving from Connecticut & elsewhere also to direct and superintend the Building of three Roe gallies on the stocks at the time under the directions of three ship carpenters. I continued in command untill taken the fever & ague and Colo. Wynkoop recovered so as to command himself I obtained a furlow from Gen[l]. Gates to ride south for the recovery of my health I therefore left camp and proceeded on South untill I arrived at the Head Quarters of General Washington near Kingsbridge at the house of my kindsman Colo. James Van Cortlandt the day the British landed at Throgs Neck where a partial Ingagement took place and the Gen[l]. said he had lost about Thirty Men. I remained a few days as aid to the Commander in Chief and paid a visit to Lieut. Colo. [Frederick] Weisenfels of the 2nd N.Y. Reg[t]. Colonel Ritzma being absent pretending to unwell. finding myself much relieved from the agae I took leave of Gen[l]. Washington and returned but having been overtaken with rain the fever was renewed and at Rhinebeck the Landlord of the tavern gave me Port Wine in which bitter herbs was infused that was so powerfull as to deprive me of understanding for ten minutes which much allarmed my friend Mr. Bell, and also the Landlord fearing I would never recover but thank God I did recover, and have not been troubled with agae since that time I then returned to Scheenesboro in perfect Health. After I left

Genl. Washington the battle of the White Plains took place.[11] and the Second New York Regiment, under the commd. of Lieut. Colo. Weisenfels was Ingaged Colo. Ritsma absent about four or five miles in the rear Either from cowardice or disaffection perhaps both for he shortly after discharging many of his men Inlisted for the war absconded himself by going to the Enemy in New York, soon after which an express arrived at Scheenesboro with a commission from Congress. This commission was sent by Genl. Washington by Express and was of his own direction having been furnished by Blanks from Congress signed by John Hancock President, for him to fill up as he thought proper, appointing me Colo. of the Second New Yord Reg^t. Dated 30 of Novr. 1776.[12] I then after taken an affectionate leave of Colo. Wynkoop set away in serch of my Regiment. Passing through New Jersie with my servant and friend Mr. Seabring I was near being captured by the Enemy at Pluckamin. I passed from a friends House near Pluckamin who sheltered me a night to New Germantown and saw my sister Catherine a few days before she lay in with the birth of her Eldest son Theodore. I then proceeded on crossing the Delaware, and arrived at the cross road in Bucks County, in the State of Pennsylvania in the Evening of the 24th Decr. The next morning my horse was foundered in such a bad manner as not to proceed in the course of the day Capt. Benj. Pelton of the Second N.Y. Reg^t. came and I suspecting that the capture of the Hessins at Trenton was contemplated by Genl. Washington I took my servants horse and with the Capt. proceeded towards Trenton as storms of hail, snow and rains came on and I lost my way but seeing after some time a light I made a House where a Quaker lived and he informid me that I was three miles from Trenton and perhaps might get lost again but was welcome to remain with him I did so and at the break of day heard the fireing which soon terminated in the capture of the Enemy I saw the prisoner[s] and Colo. Weisenfels informed me that Genl. Washing[ton] had order'd him to Fishkill in order to recruit the reg^t. and was then on his march for that purpose. I told him to proceed and after My Horse recovered I would follow and join him which I did after making a short visit in Philadelphia and passing through Morris Town paying my respects to the Com^{dr} in Chief after the Battle at Prince Town on which account as well as the Capture of the Hessians at Trenton I had the pleasure to Congratulate him altho I had not the good fortune to be present on parting from the General he directed me to use exertion to recruit and discipline my Reg^t. so as to be ready for active service in the insuing spring.[13] I then proceded onto Fishkill and sent out recruiting parties who Inlisted several men but not equal to my expectations however I was ordered in the spring of 1777 to Peekskill together with the fourth Reg^t. now under the Command of Colo. Henry B. Livingston who was promoted upon the resignation of Colo. Wynkoop. It was not long before a number of British Ships and transports appeared and landed a considerable force much superior to our troops when Genl. McDougall who commanded ordered our Troops to take post on Gallows Hill about two miles in the rear. Which movement permitted the Enemy to effect their object which was to destroy the stores which we

40

could not move and burnt a schooner which belonged to me and worth \$750 for which I could never obtain compensation they remained untill we received a Reenforcement under Lt. Colo. [Marinus] Willet who made a successfull attack on their advance Guard when they retired to the ships & went away. Shortly after on the arrival of parts of Colo. [John] Chandler and [John Durkee of Connecticut] Durgee's Reg^{ts}. from the Eastern States I was ordered with a Select Battalion to cross the Hudson and proceed on the West Side of the Town of Bergan opposite to the City of New York capture the Enemies Guards if any found in my rout of which I did surprise one Sergts. Guard but captured only 3 men in or Near the Town, and brought off all the Black Cattle & Horses out of the power of the Enemy to a considerable number without sustaining any loss much to the approbation of the Generals McDougal and Major Genl. Putnam[14] whose ade de Camp Colo. Aron Bur[15] Informed me that during my absence Colo. Livingston had been ordered on command to the White Plains with his reg^{t}. and many of mine but had left our Tents with a small guard and that Genl. Putnam's orders was that I should take the remaining Men leaving our Tents standing as Livingston had done and follow him I answered as I was the Eldest in Rank it was using Colo. Livingston very unkind to superceed him before he committed any fault. he answered that the Genl. wold write a letter of appologe for I was better acquainted with the County and I must proceed. I collected the Men to the Number of about 150 & officers and marched that afternoon hoping to surprise a Gally at Tellers point which I should have accomplished that Night if the man who was to bring Cattle to have been taken on board had arrived in time he did not and I was disappointed I then proceeded on and after Colo. Livingston rec^d. the letter Genl. Putnam sent requested that he might go to head Quarters[16] and procure an order for a board of Officers to Settle our Rank I consented and he left me in Command of about 500 rank & file and soon reinforced by a Capt. [Samuel B.] Webb and a troop of 36 Horse and a Cap^{ts}. Comp^y of 9 months men making my command of about 600 Effective Men.

During my Command on the lines opposing a line of Redoubts extending from Morris Seanea [Morrisania] to the North River on the hights contiguous to Each other amounting to five in Number. and Fort Washington about 3 miles nearer to New York amounting about 2,500 Men in all. and my nearest reinforcement 25 miles distant to Pecks Kill and my Command at no time more than ten Miles Distant from them and frequently in sight of one of the redoubts caused my duty to be Exceeding Severe shifting my quarters often for if they could assertain where to find me at Night in a few hours they might surround and attack me with three times my Number but they could not find an opportunity.[17] In day light I always defyed them thus I kept them within their works. thus for seven Weeks I remained guarding the Neutral ground and once allarming all their redoubts at Day break and one of them at another time. One Morning a Mr. Williams Son of Erasmus Williams came to me in East Chester said he had been a prisoner in the New Goal New York several Months but was sent out by an aid of Genl. How on his

promise to carry a letter to Gen[l]. Burgoyn which he took
from a fold where it was sewed in his coat. in the words
following on a small piece of Silk paper—

> To Gen[l]. Burgoyn—
>   Our destination is Changed instead
> of going to S.D.—we shall in three days sail
> for B.N.   Regulate your conduct
> accordingly

Howe

I asked if Gen[l]. How knew that his Father was one of the
State Convention of New York he said he had informed
him—but he gave no writing and his determination was
to carry the letter to the first officer he found.[18] I sent
him to Gen[l]. Putnam & never saw him after. Shortly after
I received an order to attend head Quarters at B.[ound]
Brook to have Rank settled between me and Livingston. I
set off immediately cross'd Kings ferry and met near it a
person who informed me that head Quarters was passing
thro Smiths Clove but as I might find the road filled with
troops passing, I might by a short road thro the mountains arrive at Jones Tavern as soon as their advance
could. I did so and about sunset saw Gen[l]. Green & Knox
Incam[p]ing, who detained me.[19] And before I retired to
sleep I told them of Williams and the letter which I sent to
Gen[l]. Putnam who showed them the resolves of Congress
as to York.[20] In the morning they both accompanyed me
to head Quarters where we found Gen[l]. Washington at
Breakfast with a great Number of officers—Gen[l]. Green

sat with his Excellency some short time and retired from the table shortly Genl. Green returned & sent me to the Commander in Chief who made Enquiry respecting my command in Westchester on the lines if I had seen a fleet sail up the Sound I answered that I had two or three hundred shallops escorted by an arm'd Brig & Schooner going to Loy'd Neck for forrage for the Fleet distined to the Chesepeake & then mentioned the letter of Williams and wish'd the Court of Enquiry respecting Livingstons rank might take place as I was anxious to return to my Command. he answered as to the Rank it is already settled I wish you immediately to return to your Command which [I] did after taken lieve of the Gen^{ls}. Green and Knox. On my return that morning I met Colo. Livingston and to his Enquiries I referred him to Genl. Washington who had sent me back to my Command so we parted—and the Army I soon heard was marching towards Philadelphia.

Shortly after my arrival on the Lines I received Orders[21] to march to Albany which I performed by first marching by Land to fishkill where we received a Small supply of Necessaries and Embarked on Board Sloops having both the 2^d & 4th Reg^{ts}. under my command and passing Albany Incamped with the Hamshier troops above the Cohoes falls at a place called Loudans ferry where I remained two days and was ordered to advance to the relief of Fort Stanwix now Besieged by St. Leg^{er} a British officer and Indians.[22] Genl. Poor[23] permitted me to take his Wagons as far as Schenectady where they returned to him, I then applied to Henry Glenn the Quarter Master[24] but was detain'd almost all day Sunday

44

before I could proceed however I marched on untill information was received that the Enemy had retired and Genl. Arnold was returning. L^t. Colo. Willet had made a sally from the Fort and harrassed the rear of the Enemy &c. I then was order'd to join Genl. Poor & the N. Hamshier Troops at Van Schacks Island[25] and continued annexed to that Brigade on our advance to Still Water where our Army made a stand to oppose Burgoyns Army now advansing but made a stand at Saratoga. Our army was incamped over Right on the River and Extending west Morgans Rifle Men the extream and Poors Brigade next making part of Genl. Arnolds command.[26]

[from margin]
17 Sepr.

One Day at Dinner with Genl. Arnold we was Informed that the Enemy had a reconetring Gun boat that proceeded Every night down the River in Sight of our advance guard and then returned upon which I observed If I was permitted to take a command of my men I would that Night capture them if a few Battoes with muffled oars could be fitted for me He answered prepare the men four Boats is at your service I proceeded as far up as fish Creek where I concealed my Boats and Waited the approach of the Gun Boat which did not arrive the reason was the Enemy had the day previous advanced from Saratoga and was Incamped south West from Blind Mores at whose house about half mile from me they had an advance Guard which my patroling officer discovered

45

Philip Van Cortlandt

I then resolved to surprise that Guard not knowing that
their Army was near I moved to the South West in Order
to Surround them which brough[t] me to a fence where I
halted my men and in order to assertain the best place to
make my attack on the Guard I advanced in Company
with Mathew Clarkson since made a General[27] into the
field the Morning being Very Foggey I did not see the
Centinels of the Enemy untill I had passed and was
challenged but an Owl croaking deceived the Centinel
and we stood still untill I discovered we were near the
Tents of the Enemy who were lighting up their fires as
far as I could discover, and was certain all their army was
there with their wright wing Extending S. West a considerable distance. I then retired silently to the Road I had
left near the River & stoped at a House on an Emenance
which was empty on a rising ground and sent a non
com[d]. officer Express to inform Gen[l]. Arnold and Poor
and Colo. Morgan that the Enemy was advansing so that
they might make arrangements Immediately to check
their advance which was done for Colo. Morgan had a
schirmish with their advance Guard the same day which
had the desired effect of forceing them to the left nearer
the River and more in our front. which was a fortunate
circumstance for had they that day passed our left they
might by a forced march proceeded to Albany for they
would have had possession of the Hight all the way and
we must have approach them with disadvantage but as it
was the next day we met their advance on Equal ground
and a Severe Engagement was the consequence. I am
happy to say that my discovery of the Enemys advance
saved the capture of the City of Albany.[28]

46

On the forenoon of the 19th Septr. the Enemy was Discovered moving towards our left and the action commenced first with Colo. Morgans Riflemen and reinforced by Regiments one after another (as the enemy also reinforc'd) untill the Battle became very general altho conducted by the Colonels untill about two oclock. My Reg^t. was order to march on keeping to the left in order to oppose their Right and to engage If I found it necessary and if I did that the Reg^t. commanded by Colo. Livingston who had join'd me but 2 days before, should reinforce me, this order was given me first by Genl. Poor on my parade, and as I was marching also by Genl. Arnold. I discovered their advance far from their Main Body And was determined to attack them and arrest their progress, and sent by the Adjutant L^t. [Nehemiah] Marshall to inform Colo. Livingston and direct him to support me which order he disobeyed and fil'd off to the Right leaving me to contend first with the Heshians advance of Riflemen which I defeated and who ran off but their place was Instantly supplied by the British Light Infantry whom we fought upwards of an hour at which time the Heshians had rallied and gained my left and finding it necessary to fall back with my left so as to prevent their gaining it and to oppose my front to both in case they persisted the sun having now set and my position a favorable one on a footpath which I had observed at the foot of falling ground, at least three feet lower than the level I had fought them on and had time to direct my officers to wait their approach it being now dark, and not fire untill the Enemy did and then direct below the flash of the Enemies fire which was done and proved suc-

47

cessfull as the Enemies fire went over our heads and our fire had full effect they being very near before they discovered us. I suppose not more than four or five rods—my loss of Killed and Wounded was 2 out of 11. Colo. Silley [Joseph Cilley of First New Hampshire] of our Brigade by the field return made the next day, was one out of seven—and his was more than any other Reg^t. Ingaged except mine and he fought from the first of the action being near to Colo. Morgan when it commenced—after my fire had Injured the Light Infantry we soon parted he [the commander of the Light Infantry] marched to their Incampment and I returned to mine, so we Informed each other at Albany when I met him after the Surrender he having a parole and I leave of absence for a few days and he told me the last fire Injured him very severely more than any all the day.

The Enemy did not attempt any further movement untill the 7th day of October when they advanced and was met by our army and a very severe Ingagement took place I being yet with Poors Brigade and advancing the Enemy retiring towards their Battery as the Hessians were towards theirs. General Arnold now in the field and in sight of their nine gun Battery sent his Aid to the right ordering Genl. Poor to bring his men into better order as we were pursuing this order arrested our progress and prevented our taken the British Battery in less than ten minutes as we should have Intered it almost as soon as the British, as Morgan did that of the Hessians which Arnold discovered after Sending the above order to Genl. Poor, and as he had also Sent one other order to the left by his other aid, he now rode as fast as he could to counteract his own orders as he could hurrying on the left and Entered the Hessian Battery where he was wounded— finding it to late after the British had gained their battery and rallied after their panick and could again fire their Cannon at us, which they could not do when they were running before us we found it to late and had orders to retire to our Incampment it being near Night.[29] The next morning our Brigade was order'd out at daybreak and found that the Enemy was gone from the Battery and had retired towards their left keeping possession of high lands near the river and defended by Works and Cannon mounted near which Gen[l]. Lincoln was wounded. the following night they retreated to Saratoga where they surrendered a few days afterwards.[30] As no further fighting could be expected there I accompanied the Adj[t]. Gen[l]. Wilkinson[31] to Albany and remained untill the arrival of Gen[l]. Poors Brigade who had orders with 2 Brass 24-pounders to proceed down the Hudson to annoy the Fleet and army which were burning Kingston and Houses as far up as Red Hook[32]

The Brigade March'd near the river until we found that the Enemy had retired we then took the main Road Near to Kinderhook, and upon Gen[l]. Poor being taken sick and unable to com[d] & I being the Eldest officer marched to Fish Kill and delayed a few days for the men to cure for the Itch in the Barracks at that place with hogs fat and Brimstone, the York Troops in the Upper and the Hampshier troops in the lower Barracks. going one Evening to Visit a friend I had to pass the Lower Barracks where the New Hampshire troops were stationed when coming within sight I met several soldiers Bearing

49

Philip Van Cortlandt

in a Blanket Capt. Beal[33] one of the Officers Wounded of which he died the next day. On Enquiry I found he had attempted to stop the Troops who had mutinied and was on the march headed by a Serjeant whom the Capt. Ran through the Body with his Sword and the Serjeant as he fell fired and shot the Capt. so they both died. In the confusion I came and had the address to restore order by alluring them first back to their parade by the Barracks which was near, and then in a long harrang or Preachment pointing out the Impropriety of their conduct and promise of Pardon When the Genl. should arrive. I succeeded in having my order obeyed when I sent them to their Barracks. The Genl. did not overtake me untill we arrived in Pennsylvania where we joined the Army under Genl. Washington. We remained at White Marsh untill the Enemy came out to Chesnut Hill where after some skirmishing and the loss of my friend Major Morris[34] of Colo. Morgans Rifle men we march'd and Crossed the Schoolkill and halted at Valley Forge, Shortly after our arrival it pleased his Excellency General Washington to send me with a Battalion on the lines to a place called Radner Meeting House 9 Miles from the City of Philadelphia and about 24 Miles advance of the Incampment at Valley Forge where I remained a considerable time when relieved and as soon as it was assertained that the Enemy intended to leave Philadelphia Genl. Hand the Adj^t. Genl. came and Informed me that I was to remain when the army marched, and to have the Command of & to superintend the Incampment. This I told him could not be for the Roster could not so soon after my command at Radner on the lines bring me again for

50

duty and Informed him that I would go and make my complaint to the Commander in Chief. He smiled and said do so. I went but after saying what I thought sufficient respecting an Ingagement &c., was convinced that it was his selection saying to me Sir this is an important command—&c. &c. And the Gen[l]. further observed that it was not always Convenient to have recourse to the Military Roster when a confidential officer was wanted for a particular purpose.[35]

When the army marched there was upwards of 3000 men left in the Incampment and at the Hospitals, of which number I sent off about 1500 the rest being truly so unwell as not to be able. There I remained during the Battle at Monmouth Court House[36] my Reg[t]. was ingaged and behaved well & I could have been happy if present, but was doing what the Gen[l]. had directed & of course Doing my duty. The Fever raged violently and I lost my friends Doc[r]. Haviland and Cap[t]. Ryker, my old faithful servant and soldier Mr. Lent, besides many others the fever resembled the yellow fever. After forwarding my Returns to his Excellency & being relieved by Colo. Craig of the Pennsylvania line I took a turn to Visit the City of Philadelphia on my way to join my Reg[t]. which I found Incamped with the main army at the White Plains—this was during Gen[l]. Sullivan and Gen[l]. Lafayettes Expedition on Rhode Island[37] and on our retiring, while we lay at Fredericksburg I applied for a furlow to visit my friends the Gen[l]. said when Colo. Livingston came to camp he would Indulge me & asked me to Dine with him the next day. I came and the Gen[l]. informed me that Colo. Livingston had arrived and altho he been absent almost all the campaign came to ask lieve of absence. When the Gen[l]. refused he took his commiss[n] from his pocket and handed it to the Gen[l]. who altho he felt Indignant at such behaviour replied It is not my practice to receive resignations but you are at liberty to go and resign your commission to Congress, and said he has just left me for that purpose. And on obtaining a furlough I paid a Visit to see my friends for a few days when being informed by Gov[r]. Clinton that he had requested of Gen[l]. Washington to Send my Reg[t]. to guard the frontiers where Brant the Indian was making depredations having already Burnt and destroyed several Houses and murdered men women & children. I immediately went to my Reg[t]. now near Poughkeepsie and proceeded across the North River as far as Rochester in Ulster County and placed a guard at Laghawack where I had a Blockhouse and caution'd my men so as effectually to guard the frontiers in that County during the winter 1778 & 1779.[38]

In the Spring of 1779 having information that Brant was stationed at Coke house on the Delaware I took about Two hundred and fifty Men and Set off to surprise him however on the March an Express from Gen[l]. Washington overtook me with orders to proceed to Fort Pen in the State of Pennsylvania there to receive orders from Gen[l]. Sullivan.[39] I returned and was preparing for my March first sending for the Militia to take my place this was the 3d day of April in the morning as I was about marching from my incampment having called in my guard from the Blockhouse at Laghawack. I discovered smoaks rising from the Village about six Miles South and a Lad sent from its vicinity informed that the Indians were there burning and distroying—it was occasioned by two of my men deserting in the mountains when I received the order to return for they went to Brant and informed him that I was order'd away and he Expected that I was gone for it took several days before I had received waggons, &c. and for Colo. Cantine⁴⁰ to come in with the Militia who arrived in the course of that day. On my approach Brant ran off—he had about 150 Indians and as I approached him he being on the Hill Seeing me leaning against a pine tree waiting my [orders for] the closing up of my men he ordered a Rifle Indian to kill me but he overshot me the Ball passing three inches over my head. I then persued him but could not overtake him as he ran thro a Large Swamp beyond the Hill and Colo. Cantine being also in persuit I returned not having any prospect of overtaking him. The 2d day after pursued my March to fort Pen as order'd by the Comm^r. in Chief and there received Genl. Sullivans orders who sent me reinforcements to make a Road thro the Wilderness to Wilkesbarry on the Susquehanna being thirty miles and passing the Great Swamp which duty was performed with 600 men in 30 days. On my arrival I took post advanced of the Troops under the command of Genl. Hand and Waited the arrival of Genl. Sullivan who march'd on the Road I had made with Genl. Maxwells and Genl. Poor's Brigades.⁴¹ Our Army proceeded up the River Susquahanna to Tioga Point, where I was order'd to meet Gen. Clinton who was on his march from Lake Otsago and Join'd him at Owego, & accompanied him to Tioga.

Philip Van Cortlandt

After some skirmishing with the indians at Sche-
mung we arrived near Newtown where Brant & Butler
had determined to make their Stand and oppose our
further progress if possible the action Commenced
at sunrise first with Genl. Hands Rifle Men and Reinforced by Maxwell and Poor's Brigades untill about 9
oclock when Genl. Clintons Brigade was Ordered to the
Right of the whole where we had to mount the Hill which
was mostly occupied by the Indians. I requested of Genl.
Clinton to permit me to Charge with Bayonets as soon as
I gain'd the Height on the flank of the Indians he con-
sented and ordered the charge to be made he leading the
first Reg^t. himself and I the 2d which Ended the Battle in
five minutes. They ran and left their Dead which they
seldom do, unless obliged to leave them and here they
was. Thus ended the Battle at Newtown in which not a
man of the New York Brigade was either killed or
wounded altho Several men in the other Brigades.

The army then advanced thro Catherines Town and
between Seneca and Cayuga Lakes and forded the outlett of Seneca thro Geneva Canandaihgua to Haneyau
Lake, where we Incamped and make a Cross way over
the Outlett. Here I took 9 catfish which was a great relief
for our mess had our scanty provision of 3 days stolen
from us two nights before which was truly a misfortune
as the Whole Army had been on less than half allowance
long before we came to Tioga. Here the Genl. sent Lieut.
Boyd[42] to make discovery and take Nanyous my favorite
Indian as his guyd and a few men but Boyd took also a
serjt. corpl. & 16 Men with him and proceed to a Small
Town near the prarary flats and in the Morning sent 2

54

Men back but remained untill the Indians began to appear and Murfee one of his men killed and Scalp'd one of them and advised Boyd to return but he remained to long and at last was persued untill near our Incampment he met Butler with his party who had been on the hill in our front Expecting to Ambuscade and fire on our advance after crossing the outlett. It was there I met Murfee who had with him two scalps which he had taken from two Indians he had killed that day the first in the Morning the other about 5 Minutes before he met me from the Indian who was persuing him after he left L^t. Boyd whose party Wendall killed and sckalped on the Hill my Friendly Indian being one of them not a mile from where he met me but Boyd & his serjt. they took prisoners with the intent to sacrifice at Night as they did and who we found killed tomhawked sckalped & their heads cut off lying on the ground where they had their dance. Here we found one hundred and twenty Houses all which we Burnt and Destroyed their corn as we had done all before we arrived there the Army then returned the Enemy having fled to Niagary where we afterwards heard they suffered greatly many died in short our Expedition was their compleat overthrow. On our return I went to see the Cayuga Lake and return'd to Newtown when the Genl. Sent me with a Command up the Tioga River and passed the painted Post &c. and return'd to Newtown but the Army had Marched to the point where I came up with them and we proceed to Eastown, when I was sent to Sussex and Warwick then thro Pumpton to Morristown where we hutted. Colo. Gansivort separated from the Army near Geniva and went to Albany. My Reg^t. Con-

55

tinued at Morristown all Winter first in Tents untill the snow was deep before we got into Huts which we made of Logs.

Genl. Arnold being under arrest for improper conduct in Philadelphia while he commanded there I was one of the Court martial. M. G. Howe President and there was also on that court four officers who had been at Ticonderoga when Colo. Hasen was called on for trial as before related and we were for Cashiering Arnold but were Overruled and he was sentised to be reprimanded by the Commander in Chief. If all the court had known Arnolds former Conduct as well as myself how he and his Brigade Major had Robed Merchants in Montreal he would have been Dismissed from serving any longer in our Army for he would have been cashiered if so he would never have had the Command at West Point & Major Andre might have lived untill this day.[43]

The Reg^t. remained at Morris Town untill the Spring of 1780 and was then marched towards the Northern frontiers in the State of New York and having passed thro the Manor of Cortlandt Saw My friends at Peeks Kill and then to Nine Partners where my Father and his family were obliged to remove from Rhinebeck as Colo. Livingston would not suffer him to remain any longer. I then joined the Reg^t. and went to Fort Edward on the North River and was in a few days relieved by Colo. Warner I then proceeded to West Point and Incamped on the West part in June 1780 and as there was some Expectation of an attack from the Enemy I took post on the Mountain West of Fort Putnam this was in June & July when I was selected as one of the Colonels to

Command in a Selected Reg^t. of Infantry under Major Genl. Lafayette, who was returned from France and had Two Brigades—the first comm^d. by Genl. Hand with Colo. Stewart of Pennsylvania. Colo. Ogden of Jersey and myself of New York the other Brig^e. by Genl. Poor, with Colo. Shepherd of Massachusets. Colo. Swift of Connecticut and Colo. Germat a French officer together with Colo. Henry Lee and his Troop of Horse, and a Majors Command of Artilery.⁴⁴ Major Genl. Lafayette with his Division was stationed in front of the Main Army at Tapan on the West side of the Hudson where the British Ad^t. Genl. Major Andre was executed as a Spy. Our Division made a movement to Bergan near Powles Hook but the Enemy kept close in New York and their ships—so that we had no oppertunity of Ingaging them we also approached them towards Staten Island Marching and returning without effecting anything of Importance & so Ended the Campaign.

In the month of Novr. 1780—the M. G. Lafayettes division being order'd to join their respective lines of the Army of course the Division was seperated—and the Genl. Sent to join the Southern Army in Virginia—I proceeded to Albany where my Reg^t. was ordered by Genl. James Clinton to be cantooned in the town of Schenectady and where I went with them and placed my Men in the Barracks myself at Mr. Daniel Cammells, and the officers at private Houses which was obtained with some Directly [Difficulty]. As the first Reg^t. had been there winter previous and their billeting not as yet paid for.

In December the New York Line of the five Regi-

57

ments[45] was to be incorporated into Two, the first & third to be under the Command of Colo. Van Schaick and the Second, fourth and fifth, J[n]. Livingstons, & that part of Spencers belonging to this State was to be under my Command, and I was ordered to incorporate them they being now at Different places on the frontiers on the Mohawk River, the old fourth stationed at Fort Schuyler. I was order to that place and my now L[t]. Colo. Cochran[46] permitted on furlough. There I remained untill his return when I returned to Albany and while absent the Barracks took fire and burnt up the fort. When Gen[l]. Clinton order'd me back and altho severely afflicted with sore Eyes however I went and Distroyed all the Fort and brought off the Cannon &c., to Fort Harkimer and was ordered to Build a new Fort having Major Ville Franch[47] as Ingineer, after looking out the place clearing of the Timber & brush and a few 9 months men under Cap[t]. Elsworth[48] join'd me I was ordered to repair to Albany and call in all my Officers and Men from the different stations. Viz. Fort Plain Stone Arrabia, Johns Town, Schoharry, &c., &c. leaving Capts. Elsworth, & Moody[49] at Herkimer and before I arrived at Schenectady I was Informed of the Death of Cap[t]. Elsworth who was killed by a scout of Indians while he was out on a fishing party.

All my Regiment having joined at and Near Schenectady I marched and Incamped on the Pattroons Flats. I had then the largest and most healthy Reg[t]. in America not Excepting French, English or Germains and a fine Band of Musick. Here I had to remain for the compleating of 34 Boats now building there for the purpose as reported to take our army from Elizabeth Town to Staten Island as soon as the French Fleet should appear off Sandy Hook in order to take New York.[50]

Count Roshambeau with the French forces having March'd from R. Island had advanced to the lines in Westchester County near Kingsbridge some part of Our Army already in the State of New Jersey, and all things ready the French fleet daily expected I rec[d]. orders to take the Boats Reg[t]. & bagging, &c. and proceed down the Hudson to Stoney Point.[51] Landed and Incamped, remained there while the French passed and some time after, untill information that Gen[l]. Washington was himself at the ferry and wished to see me. Upon approaching him He took my [me] by the arm and went some distance on the road and gave me his orders both written and verbill, which was to March to Chatham in N. Jersey taken all the boats Intrenching tools &c. and proceed with deliberation Informing him daily of my progress for which purpose he sent a Dragoon every day, as my Command was of great importance being the Rear Guard of the Army.[52] Upon my arrival at Pumpton Plains he altered my rout but on my request permitted me to take a more circuitous one through Parsipany— the road being better passing Mr. Lott & Beaverhout[53] —but not pass the junction of the Morristown Road with the Chatham untill the next morning then Instead of going to the Latter I must pass thro Morris and make an Expeditious March to Trenton and Enjoined secrecy for three days. I did as ordered after Dining with Mr. Lott & spending the afternoon with his family my camp being near his House & marched by Day Break next morning 24 miles, instead of 8 or 9 as customary from Kings ferry. Arriving about 3 miles from Trenton I was ordered to Incamp for all the army to pass me and then took my Boats to Trenton and Embarked my Reg^t. and proceeded on the Delaware. To Philadelphia where I halted one day to accommodate my officers who wanted some articles of Clothing &c.—then proceeded to Markees Hook where I remained a few days for the Army to pass and my men to wash their clothes then proceeded on passing Wilmington to the head of Elk, where I left the Boats and Marched by land to Baltimore where I Encamped on the Hill being a part of Mr. Howards Farm now a part of Baltimore City. After remaining a few days and moving to Fells Point on board of shallops sailed to James River in the State of Virginia and landed at Colledge Landing then march'd to Williamsburgh where I was made exceeding happy to meet my General Lafayette who had a Command of Light Infantry, and Colo. Hamilton[54] and my Major N. Fish[55] was selected to join his Command who with Colo. Schammel,[56] my old & particular friend in his advance proceeded to Invest Yorktown where the Renowned and Haughty Commander of the British army had Intrenched himself.

Colonel Schammel advanced in Sight of their advanced Redoubts which they abandoned in the course of the night. I being ordered out the next morning with a strong Picket Guard to relieve Colo. Schammel I found his men and relieved them but the Colo. had before my arrival observed that they had retired from the Poplar Tree Redoubt to road in front, and mistook a British pattrol of Horse for our Men was under the necessaty of

surrendering when one of their dragoons coming up
fired and wounded the Colo. after his Surrender but
whether the Dragoon new of the Surrender being behind him I cannot say but from all the Information I
could obtain it was after his Surrender. The Colo. was
first taken to the Town then paroled to Williamsburg
where he died in our Hospital and buried with the hon-
ors of War.[57] That morning the Commander in Chief
with almost all the General officers came to my picket and
was in my front while I was seated on the platform of the
poplar redoubt Viewing their Battery about one mile
distant, the enemy fired over their Heads and cut
branches of the Tree which fell about me, but as the
Generals did not move the Second Ball struck directly in
my front Struck and went in the ground about 3 rods
before the Generals (had it raised it must have passed
thro the Cluster and have killed Several) when they all
retreated except the Commander in Chief who remained
with his spying glass observing their works and altho he
remained sometime alone directly in their View and in
my front they did not fire again. The Gen[l]. then came
toward me which observing I rose and mett him when
after some Remarks and Enquiries he directed me to
keep my men as they were at present disposed of out of
sight of the Battery untill the Evening then to surround
the Town with my centinels from the Redoubt which was
to the right all the way to the York River and that Baron
Viominal[58] with the French pickets should do the same to
the left. And the next morning they found themselves
Completely Surrounded by a Chain of Active and Vigil-
ant Centinels. Preparations were now made and the fol-

61

lowing night the Army made in the range of the Centinels a Compleat Intrenchment which covered our Men and gave facility to our preparing our Battiry of Cannon which when in order, the first gun which was fired I could distinctly hear pass thro' the Town being on the line directly in front near the poplar redoubt, and our Battery being on or near the river on our right. I could hear the Ball strike from House to house, and I was afterwards Informed that it went thro the one where many officers were at dinner and over the Tables discomposing the Dishes and Either Killed or Wounded the one at the head of the Table and I also heard that gun was fired by the Comm^r. in Chief, who was designedly present in the battery for the express purpose of putting the first match.

The Enemy having two Redoubts about 350 yards advance of the line and Batteries which surrounded the Town and which was an anoyance to our progress, it was determined to take them by storming. The one was assign'd for Genl. Lafayetts light Infantry the other for Baron Vaominil with the French granidiers. Colo. Hamilton with Major Fish and other officers and men of the American Light Infantry advanced against the Right one near the River, and took it in a few minutes. When the Genl. Lafayette sent to the French Baron information who returned answer he had not but would in five minutes which I believe he did—both the above were brilliant exploits Crown'd the Assailants with Everlasting honor particularly as they extended Mercy to Every one who solicited it after entering the Works, which was not the case when Baylors horse was surprised.[59] After the two Redoubts were taken we advanced our lines in their range and the next morning I advanced the York Brigade which I then comm^d. with Drums and Coulours flying and Carried arms up to the Redoubt which Baron Vaominil had taken which Insulting movement drew on the resentment of our Enemies who fired an insessant shower of Recashe Shells without doing any injury to us only killed a Frinch granadier in my front and a Virginian retiring on my left. One of the shot as I entered the Intrenchment cut its upper part and almost covered me and the Marquis Steuben[60] who was meeting me when he directed me to stop my musick which I did and the firing ceased. When I came to the Redoubt it was necessary to Cut away a part to get a Mortar to play on the Enemy when one of Capt. Van Denburghs[61] Fatigue Party was killed the first stroke [for he was] struck by a 9 lb Ball which carried off his thigh close to his Body. On seeing this a volunteer was called for as the case was desperate when a soldier who had been disgraced as he told me without cause, took the place and performed the work altho during its Execution three Balls were fired at him all of which came within six inches one almost Covered his head with sand. His name was Peter Christian Vouch and his brother is my Neighbour at Peekskill. Another remarkable occurrance Serg^t. Brown was leaning over the embankment looking at the Enemies Battery when Capt. Vandenburgh order him down and as he slid down the Ball that was intended to kill him and which would have passed thro his body if he had remained passed over his head and either the Wind or the Sand as it passed without breaking his skull or skin produced his death in an Instant as he fell dead in the trench no mark but bloodshod head and face. Here one of my small drummers asked me if he might remove a Vest from a British dead soldier who I had ordered to be buried in which he found Eleven guineas so he was well paid for his attention to the dead soldier. The siege was now continued with Cannon and Morters on both sides. I have counted 13 shells flying in the air at night at one time going to and from the Enemy.

One night the Enemy (I suppose to save Appearances as a point of honor) made a Sortie on a French Battery by surprise killed some and spiked the guns but was soon obliged to retire with some loss. They also attempted to cross the river at Gloster with all the Army and force their way by land but a storm arising they were obliged to return; but had they Succeeded in crossing they never would have been able to rech N. York, so disperate was their situation, and at length the haughty Cornwallis sent out a Flag and asked a Suspention to give time for Negotiation of Surrender which was agreed to by Genl. Washington, on the like terms which Genl. Lincoln had obtain'd at the Surrender of Charlestown from this same Lord Cornwallis.[62] And the day when they gave up their Arms Colours &c. Genl. Lincoln had the pleasure of Conducting them to the Field of deposite much to their mortification however they performed it with more order than I Expected. The Prisoners were soon sent into the Interior and it fell to my lot (as Genl. Clinton who commanded the Division and General Daton of the New Jersey[63] Brigade were somewhat Indisposed and permited to return by water) to command the Division composed of the New York and N. Jersey Brigades, to march them by land and had the charge of 700 of the British and Hession Prisoners as far as the Town of Fredericksburgh where I delivered them to an officer of the Virginia Militia and then continued my march thro Alexandria, George Town Bladenburg Baltimore Philadelphia Trenton in New Jersie where the Troops of that State left me and I continued my march with the N. York Brigade to Pumpton where I commenced to make Hutts for our Winter accomodation. I was asked at Hanover Court House $500 for a Bowl of apple Tody but was satisfied by paying one silver Dollar.

The troops being almost distitute of Clothing, no money to purchase any and often scanted for Provisions and obliged to labour hard to make the Hutts warm and the weather Extream cold so that it was attended with difficulty and almost cruelty to keep them Exposed in the open air to hear Preaching from our Worthy Chaplain, Doc[r]. John Gannoe.[64] I therefore permitted him to Return to his family untill called for, which I found was not necessary untill the breaking up of Winter when he returned of his own pleasure and Informed me that he had received a Lecture from one of the Soldiers which he overtook as he Came near the Incampment. It appeared that the Doctor made Enquiry of the soldier how the commandent "meaning myself" the officers and Men had Injoyed health during the Winter while he was absent &c. The soldiers answer—Dear Doctor we have had Tolerable Health but hard times otherwise we have wanted almost Every thing, scanted in clothing, provisions and money and hardest of all, we have not had even the word of God to Comfort us. The Doc[r]. then gave as a reason why he was absent it being hard to oblige the men badly clad, to attend worship. True said the Soldier but it would have had been consoling to have had such a good man near us. That remark said the Doc[r]. was unanswerable Shortly after he pointed out the Soldier who was a reprobate fellow and had diverted himself with quissing the Doc[r].

The Church on the low grounds being obtain'd for Doc[r]. Gannoe to preach in on the following Sabath, on the Saturday Evening previous I let him see the Brigade return and observed it would be more pleasing if all the men were for the War but there was several Six Months and 9 Months men which I wished to Inlist. On Sunday in his Introduction to the Sermone he observed that it always gave him pleasure to preach to soldiers Especially when he had good tidings to Communicate, and he could aver of the truth that Our Lord and Sivier approved of all those ingaged in his service for the whole warfair—no 9 or 6 Months men in his service. This had a fine effect for many Inlisted shortly after to silence the pleasantry I supposed of their Companions. This was in the spring of 1782, when thinking it more expedient to Incamp the men we moved to the flat fields and there Exercised and Manuevered to great advantage in the presence of Baron Steuben who was delighted with our performances during his visit of a few days.

I omitted to mention in the above that while we continued in the Hutts His Excellency Gen[l]. Washington came with his Lady on a Visit and remained in my humble station from Saturday Evening untill Monday Morning when I sent an escort with him as a Guard on his way to New Burgh.[65]

In the summer of 1782, after General Washington & his Lady had left me for Newburgh and the French Army under the Gen[l]. Rochambeau was returning, my Command was ordered to Verplancks Point where the Army Incamped composed of the New England N. York & N. Jersey Troops the latter on the right and when the French passed on to the Peeks Kill and remained a few days Incamped the Army at V. Plancks was reviewed by the Commander in Chief accompanied by the French Generals. We were assebled in close column under the Command of Major Gen[l]. Baron Steuben and march'd as if approaching an Enemy and under a supposed Ingagement had to Display when I discovered a mistake and rectified it Instantly in such a manner as to attract the notice of all the General officers attending and gained more honor than any Reg[t]. Ingaged by my Activity in rectifying the mistake without creating a disorder under a presumed heavy fire.

This being the first and only period of the War that I was Incamped and Stationed near my own Habitation I had the pleasure of receiving the Vissits of my friends which in some measure made Amends for the Inactment of the campaign which terminated by marching to the Vicinity of New Windsor and commenced the making of Hutts for our Accomodation for the Winter near the road leading to Little Britain the residence of Gen[l]. J[s]. Clinton. The Month of January 1783, found us in Hutts of our own making as comfortable as Troops could expect without pay, scarcity of provisions at times, and also in Want of Sufficient Clothing however better than we had formerly experienced and as the Accounts of the termination of the War was gaining a belief we was Induced by the promises of Congress of future rewards to persevere in orderly discipline to the End.

As the Spring of the year came on a Signonamous [anonymous] Letter made its appearance which Caused much Uneasiness especially at Head Quarters and the Genl. came to Camp and sent for the Officers commanding Brigades and as I had the Command of the New York Line I attended with others and was happy to find a unanimous determination to support order and agreed with Genl. Washington to Suppress Every attempt at disorderly conduct, which was subsequently confirmed in a full Meeting of all the officers assembled together in the large Hall which had been Erected near the Massachusets line with a full belief that Congress would Ultimately compensate the Army for their Services & Sufferings.[66]

In the month of May the Society of the Cincinnata was organized.[67] And in June it was Resolved by the officers of the N. Y. Brigade to present Governor George Clinton with the stand of Colours and Instruments of musick belonging to the Brigade, and I was requested to present them to the Governor at his residence in the town of Poughkeepsie[68] which request was attended to and as I remained a few days in Poughkeepsie with the Governor, I found on my return to the Cantonment that almost all were gone, as only a few was left and they wanted assistance some unwell and others without the means of Removal. I myself determining to go to Croton—in the

first place purchased the Barge or Row Boat from the Q^r.
Mast^r.[69] and some Extra Provisions and hired a few Sol-
diers one of which a mulatto with his wife and child to act
as cook. I set off, and arrived at the Farm at the Mouth of
Croton River, where I was joined in a short by Cap^{ts}.
Hamtramck and Vanderburgh and also by Doc^r. Pryer
who I had Invited to stay with me untill we could go into
N. York and they were happily Employed sometimes
Gunning and fishing, &c. &c.[70]

NOTES

1. The Parliamentary Calendar Act of 1750 modified the calendar to the extent of making the day following September 2, 1752, Old Style, to read September 14, New Style. The second change modified the commencement of the legal year from March 1 to January 1. *Encyclopaedia Britannica* (Chicago, 1957), IV, 572.

2. Van Cortlandt Manor had been created under a Crown patent issued on June 17, 1697, to Stephanus Van Cortlandt. Upon his death in 1700, the lands were to be divided among his eleven surviving heirs.

    The Croton River lands were left to the oldest son, John. He died without male heirs and so the lands descended to his brother, Oliver. He died in 1708 without heirs and the land, at that point, became the property of Philip's grandfather, Philip (1683–1746). See Genealogy, pp. 19–22.

3. One of the foremost Enlightenment figures in Colonial America, Cadwallader Colden of New York was a politician, historian, botanist, mathematician, surveyor, apothecary, and practicing physician. He also established a school in the 1760s which he named after his estate, Coldengham. At the time when Philip was in attendance, the school was located in New Rochelle. An advertisement for the "Grammar School, at New Rochell" stated that it is "still continued under the tuition of Mr. ADAMS, where the liberal arts are taught (as usual) with the greatest care and assiduity. As there is no study more useful than the mathematicks, so there is none polishes and improves more the rational faculty, for it gives the mind a habit of close and demonstrative reasoning . . . ." William Adams eventually practiced medicine and died in Mt. Pleasant, Westchester, in 1819. *The New-York Gazette and the Weekly*

Mercury, June 11, 1770; Beekman Family Papers, Sleepy Hollow Restorations; Brooke Hindle, "A Colonial Governor's Family: The Coldens of Coldengham," *The New-York Historical Society Quarterly* (July 1961), XLV, No. 3, 233 ff.; Jacob Judd, "Dr. Colden's Cure," *Ibid*., pp. 251–254.

4. Pierre Van Cortlandt (1721–1814), Philip's father, was first elected to the New York Assembly in March 1768 and served in that body as the representative from Van Cortlandt Manor until 1775. He emerged as a member of the more radical wing of that body, among whom were such Revolutionary stalwarts as George Clinton, Philip Schuyler, and Philip Livingston. Not an orator, Pierre's strength lay in his administrative abilities and sense of detail. This was soon put to the test, for as the first Lieutenant Governor of the State of New York, elected in 1777, he served as the state's chief administrator while the Governor, George Clinton, fulfilled his other role as a general in the Revolutionary army. *New York Gazette and the Weekly Mercury*, 1768–1775; New York State, *Journal of the Votes and Proceedings of the General Assembly of the Colony of New-York* (New York, 1774, 1775), *passim*.

5. William Tryon served as Governor of North Carolina from 1765 to 1771, when he was transferred to New York. He was married to Margaret Wake, daughter of a wealthy Londoner.

   Edmund Fanning, born in New York, moved to Hillsboro, North Carolina upon his graduation from Yale College in 1757. He became Tryon's associate when the latter came to that colony and subsequently married the Governor's daughter. Fanning accompanied Tryon to New York, and later became an active Loyalist.

   John Watts had married Pierre Van Cortlandt's first cousin, Anne DeLancey. He served in the General Assembly and was a member of the Provincial Council at the time of the Revolution. Because of his active Loyalism his property was confiscated by the State of New York. His daughter, Ann married Archibald Kennedy, who later became the eleventh Earl of Cassilis. *D. Col. N.Y.*, VIII, 798; *DAB*, VI, 265–266; James G. Wilson and John Fiske, eds. *Appletons' Cyclopaedia of American Biography* (New York, 1889), VI, 395.

6. William Tryon was the last royally appointed governor of the Province of New York. If Philip's memory was correct as to the year of Tryon's visit to Van Cortlandt Manor, it would have had to occur prior to April 7, when the Governor departed from New York on a transatlantic voyage to England. Tryon left amidst a rising uproar by New Yorkers over the passage of the Tea Act by Parliament. While Boston's Tea Party is the more famous, New York had its own miniature Tea Party on April 22, just a fortnight after Tryon had sailed away. Bernard Mason, *The Road to Independence: The Revolutionary Movement in New York, 1773–1777* (Lexington, Ky., 1966), pp. 19–21.

7. James Ver Planck operated a general store in Van Cortlandt Manor and eventually ran his family's properties in Westchester. William Ver Planck, *The History of Abraham Isaacse Ver Planck and His Male Descendants* (Fishkill, N.Y., 1892).

8. Goose Van Schaick was Colonel of the First New York Regiment. Heitman, p. 557.

9. Even before the British army evacuated Boston in March 1776, the locale of the as yet undeclared war shifted to the Province of New York, both to the city of New York and to the northern frontier. Fort Ticonderoga at the head of Lake George had been captured by an American force on May 10, 1775, and this opened the path for an American

invasion of Canada by way of Lake Champlain, to the Richelieu River, and then to the St. Lawrence. The command of the Northern Army was placed in the hands of Philip Schuyler of Albany, while the New York City theater of operations came under the direct control of George Washington. The invasion of Canada began in a desultory fashion in September 1775 and the British invasion of New York City and harbor began during the first week of July 1776. Some recent studies which cover these campaigns are: Bruce Bliven, Jr., *Under the Guns: New York 1775–1776* (New York, 1972); Martin H. Bush, *Revolutionary Enigma: A Re-appraisal of General Philip Schuyler of New York* (Port Washington, N.Y., 1969); Don R. Gerlach, *Philip Schuyler and the American Revolution in New York, 1733–1777* (Lincoln, Nebr., 1964).

10. A wealthy merchant residing in St. Johns, Quebec, at the opening of the Revolution, Moses Hazen soon joined the American forces under Richard Montgomery in the Canadian campaign during the summer and fall of 1775. In the course of the American retreat, Hazen and Benedict Arnold had a falling out over Hazen's alleged sale of goods destined for army use. As a result, Arnold formally complained to General Philip Schuyler in June 1776 of Hazen's alleged insubordination. A military court was convened at Ticonderoga in July, and on August 7 it acquitted Hazen of the charges. The court, however, apparently felt that charges should, instead, be levied against Arnold, for General Gates reported to Congress on September 2, that "I was obliged to act dictatorially, and dissolved the Court Martial the instant they demanded General Arnold to be put in arrest."

Hazen did not soon forget this incident and later the same year he instituted charges against Arnold for slanderous statements. Another court-martial was convened in Albany early in December to hear the charges which stemmed from Arnold's remark that Hazen had sold rum destined for army use to private tavern owners in Quebec Province. Again Philip sat as a member of the court and it determined that Arnold's written statement declaring that "Colonel Hazen can best tell how much he sold" was an "aspersion of Colonel Hazen's character, and therefore think the complaint just." Force, *Archives, IV*, VI, 796–797; *V*, III, 1042.

11. After removing his forces from Manhattan Island in October, 1776, Washington established a new line of defense in Westchester County on the mainland of New York. General William Howe followed in pursuit of the Americans who were established at White Plains. On October 25, 1776, Howe began the campaign by placing his men just below White Plains. Then on the 28th, he launched an attack against a detached American wing on Chatterton Hill. Although ably defended by a force under the command of Alexander McDougall, Chatterton's Hill fell to a superior combined army of British Regulars and Hessians. Otto Hufeland, *Westchester County during the American Revolution* 1775–1783 (White Plains, N.Y., 1926), pp. 131–149.

12. In the 1775 arrangement of New York troops, four regiments were created under the following officers:

First New York
        Alexander McDougall, Col.
        Rudolphus Ritzema, Lt. Col.
Second
        Myndert Roseboom, Col.
        Goosen Van Schaick, Lt. Col.

Third

        James Clinton, Col.
        Edward Flemming, Lt. Col.

Fourth

        James Holmes, Col. (Soon replaced
        by Jacobus Wynkoop).
        Philip Van Cortlandt, Lt. Col.

After undergoing various modifications, the New York regiments were rearranged in November 1776.

First

        Goosen Van Schaick, Col.
        Cornelius Van Dyck, Lt. Col.

Second

        Philip Van Cortlandt, Col.
        Frederick Weissenfels, Lt. Col.

Third

        Peter Gansevoort, Col.
        Marinus Willet, Lt. Col.

Fourth

        Henry B. Livingston, Col.
        Benjamin Ledyard, Major

Cal. H. Mss., II, 48–50; *N.Y. in Rev.,* pp. 138–140.

13. General Washington began the march toward Trenton on the afternoon of December 25, 1776. The famous crossing of the Delaware occurred during the early hours of the 26th in the midst of a whirling storm. Washington's successful campaign produced over nine hundred Hessian prisoners. These were prisoners Philip met soon after the battle. Philip then proceeded to Philadelphia, according to the *Memoir,* and must have arrived at Washington's headquarters in Morristown after January 5, when the Ameri-

can Army returned from their successful surprise attack against the British at Princeton. Boatner, pp. 782–787; 890–894; 1112–1115.

14. Shortly after being named as Colonel of the Second New York, Philip's regiment was placed under the command of Alexander McDougall. In May 1777 Washington decided to have a Major General in charge of the Hudson Highlands and named Israel Putnam to that command. Both McDougall and Putnam seemed to share the same headquarters at Peekskill.

   Philip refers to the "Black Cattle & Horses" captured in Bergen County, New Jersey, in the spring of 1777. The *General Orders* of General Israel Putnam contain the statement that on July 8, 1777, at Peekskill, New York, the "Cattle and Sheep that were taken by Col. Courtland at Bergen to be sold at publick Vendue . . . ." Worthington C. Ford, ed., *General Orders Issued by Major-General Israel Putnam* (Brooklyn, N.Y., 1893), p. 23; Washington to Alexander McDougall, March 12, 1777, in Fitzpatrick, VII, 277–278.

15. The Vice President during Thomas Jefferson's first term in office, Aaron Burr had a distinguished career in the military service during the Revolution. After having served under Benedict Arnold, Burr was transferred to Israel Putnam's command in New York. *DAB*, III, 314–315.

16. George Washington wrote to Henry Beekman Livingston on June 1, 1777, that in regard to Livingston's complaint of not being properly treated as to rank, he would not "undertake to determine, how far injustice has been done to you, in regard to arranging any of the Colonels before you,

but it is evidently so in the case of Colonels Gansevoort and Cortlandt, as far as may be collected from the papers transmitted." Since there was a question of rank which had to be determined, Washington recommended to Livingston that, "It is therefore my wish that if you and Genl. McDougall cannot terminate your dispute amicably, that you would lodge a complaint to Genl. Putnam and desire a Court of Inquiry. This is the proper mode of proceeding, when an inferior officer thinks himself aggrieved by his superior." Washington to Henry B. Livingston, June 1, 1777 in Fitzpatrick, VII, 164–165; See fn. 2, Philip to New York Provincial Congress, August 5, 1776, p. 118.

17. Philip was placed in charge of the so-called "Neutral Ground" in Westchester County. This consisted of the territory to the north of the British lines on upper Manhattan Island and lower Westchester which then extended in a northerly direction to the American outposts above the Croton River. The Loyalist diarist, Stephen Kemble, who happened to be a distant relative to Philip through a mutual great-grandfather, noted that two American deserters who had crossed into the British lines "come from a party of 300 men under a Colonel Cortlandt posted at White Plains; they say there are no detachments nearer than PEEKSKILL where Putnam commands . . . " New-York Historical Society, *Kemble Papers, Collection for the Year* 1883 (New York, 1884), pp. 125–126.

18. It was assumed by the British command that General William Howe would provide adequate military forces from New York City to join General John Burgoyne's campaign of cutting off New England from the rest of the States by his capturing control of Lake Champlain, Albany, and the

Hudson River Valley. At the same time, Howe also was expected to seize Philadelphia and isolate Washington's army in New Jersey. It was no secret that Howe intended to invade Philadelphia sometime during that spring or summer of 1777. What the Americans did not know was that Howe had determined to reach Philadelphia by sailing from New York to the Chesapeake. Ira D. Gruber, *The Howe Brothers and the American Revolution* (New York, 1972), pp. 231–237.

19. Washington's headquarters had been moved to Bound Brook, New Jersey, some twenty miles south of Morristown. Pierre C. Van Wyck's edited version of the *Memoir* reads: "I received an order to attend headquarters (at B———.)"

Philip's manuscript *Memoir* contains a statement that he found Generals Nathanael Greene and Henry Knox preparing an encampment. Pierre C. Van Wyck's version reads: ". . . about sunset saw Generals Greene and Knox, who detained me." Pierre C. Van Wyck, ed. "Autobiography of Philip Van Cortlandt, Brigadier-General in the Continental Army," *Magazine of American History* (May, 1878), pp. 278ff.

20. In June 1777, Congress passed a number of resolutions relating to New York's claims to land in the New Hampshire territory and to supplying the soldiers and civilians of New York with salt. Worthington C. Ford, ed. *Journals of the Continental Congress, 1774–1789* (Washington, D.C., 1904–1907), VIII, 466, 509.

21. On July 30, 1777, Major General Israel Putnam ordered Philip Van Cortlandt and the soldiers under his command to join their brigades and to await further marching orders. Ford, *General Orders Issued by Major-General Israel Putnam*, p. 42.

22. While General John Burgoyne proceeded with his invasion of northern New York along Lake Champlain, a diversionary move was inaugurated by Lieutenant Colonel Barry St. Leger late in July, 1777 against the American position at Fort Stanwix. He began the attack against the fortification on August 3. Successful American raids against the encampments of St. Leger's Indian allies disheartened the Indians to the extent that they began to abandon him. One such raid was carried out by Marinus Willett and two hundred and fifty men. The British siege of Fort Stanwix was broken when Benedict Arnold arrived at the head of a relief column on August 23. Marinus M. Willett, ed. *A Narrative of the Military Actions of Colonel Marinus Willett, Taken Chiefly from His Own Manuscript* (New York, 1969 reprint of 1831 edition) pp. 43–64; Boatner, 960–963.

23. Enoch Poor of New Hampshire was elevated to the rank of Brigadier General in February, 1777. Philip sat on the court-martial over which Poor presided involving Arnold's charges against Moses Hazen. Heitman, p. 446; Boatner, pp. 880–881; and fn. 10, pp. 73–74.

24. Henry Glen was a Schenectady merchant who was a member of the Schenectady Committee of Safety. He later became the deputy quartermaster in charge of military supplies at Schenectady. He also served in Congress with Philip from 1793 until 1802. Other Henry Glen papers in addition to those described by Throop Wilder were part of the Van Cortlandt family papers until sold in 1941 at a Parke-Bernet auction. Throop Wilder, "The Glen Letters: That We May Remember," *New York History* (July, 1945), pp. 322–331; Parke-Bernet Galleries, Inc. *The Papers of The Van Cortlandt, Beck, Clinton & Caldwell Families, Public Sale Tuesday, February* 11(New York, 1941).

25. Van Schaick's Island was a small island in the Hudson River near its confluence with the Mohawk. Fortifications were constructed on the island during Burgoyne's campaign and remained in use until St. Leger's retreat from Fort Stanwix. Ruins of the fortifications were still visible in 1860. French, p. 166.

26. Daniel Morgan of Virginia created a cadre of five hundred sharpshooters in 1777 who soon became known as Morgan's Rangers. His men played a decisive role in the American victory at Saratoga.

    Enoch Poor's Brigade consisted of three New Hampshire regiments led by Joseph Cilley, George Reid and Alexander Scammel, and two New York regiments under Henry B. Livingston and Philip Van Cortlandt. Boatner, pp. 736–737; Rupert Furneaux, *The Battle of Saratoga* (New York, 1971), p. 226.

27. Matthew Clarkson of Massachusetts bore the rank of major. Philip was mistaken as to his field rank. In 1783 Clarkson was breveted a lieutenant colonel. Heitman, p. 159.

28. Ordered to transport his men to the vicinity of the confluence of the Hudson and Mohawk rivers in August 1777, Philip Van Cortlandt could not possibly know that he would soon be engaged in one of the most important battles in American history. In the midst of preparations to join General Arnold's forces who were then on their way to relieve the beleaguered American position at Fort Stanwix, Philip received word that he was to proceed instead to the area of Stillwater, some eleven miles south of Saratoga.

    In the *Memoir*, Philip vividly recalls his activities of September 17 and 18. In the course of attempting to capture a British gunboat on the Hudson River on the

80

night of the 17th, he and his men stumbled upon an advance guard of General Burgoyne's British forces at a place he designated as "Blind Mores." Upon realizing that a main enemy encampment was nearby, he immediately dispatched a non-commissioned officer to notify Generals Arnold and Poor, along with Colonel Daniel Morgan, that "the Enemy was advansing so that they might make arrangements Immediately to check their advance." Such action on his part, Philip later declared, "saved the capture of the City of Albany." Despite the fact that he fully believed that the consequence of his deeds on the night of the 17th was such that it raised the alarm which produced an American countermovement against a further British advance, there is little contemporary evidence to support his contention. The extant papers and biographies of Arnold, Poor, and Morgan make no reference to the receiving of such information from one of Van Cortlandt's men.

Furthermore, from the British accounts of the battle it becomes clear that they had not altered their line positions since the 16th of September and did not make the dramatic effort to dislodge the Americans until the 19th. Philip's regiment, occupying a position on the left flank, played a significant role in the fighting on the 19th and in the subsequent battle of Bemis Heights on October 7. Following this battle, General John Burgoyne surrendered his forces, which event had political repercussions throughout Europe. Philip certainly could claim credit for his frontline participation in these two major conflicts, but it cannot be shown that to him is due credit for having prevented Albany from falling into Burgoyne's control. Furneaux, *The Battle of Saratoga,* pp. 153ff.; Ward, II, 506–511; Don Higginbotham, *Daniel Morgan: Revolutionary Rifleman* (Chapel Hill, N.C., 1961), p. 65; Thomas Anbury, *Travels Through the Interior Parts of America* (Boston, 1923), I, 241–245.

29. Whether Philip's blatant animosity toward Benedict Arnold can be traced to the latter's treasonable actions concerning West Point cannot be ascertained. His bitterness toward Arnold surfaces, however, in his description of Arnold's activities on the afternoon of October 7, 1777, during the battle of Bemis Heights in the Saratoga campaign. Philip portrays Arnold as the officer who "arrested our progress and prevented our taken the British Battery in less than ten minutes as we should have Intered it almost as soon as the British." Recent military historians would not come to the same conclusion. Mark M. Boatner states, "Arnold's contribution was in following up on the initial success and, by the capture of the Breymann Redoubt [to the right and forward of Philip Van Cortlandt's position], making Burgoyne's entire position untenable." Christopher Ward, in his famous study of the Revolution, goes even further by declaring that to Arnold and Col. Morgan "belongs the credit for the victory." Boatner, pp. 977–978; Ward, II, 530–531.

30. The surrender by General John Burgoyne at Saratoga is known as the Convention of Saratoga. Under its terms, the British were to surrender their weapons and then return to England under the pledge that they would never fight again in America. The Continental Congress was unhappy with these terms and did not permit the troops to return to England for fear that they would release other troops for America. Marshall Smelser, *The Winning of Independence* (Chicago, 1972), pp. 198–199.

31. Later to be a chief witness in the Burr conspiracy trial, James Wilkinson was a soldier with a ready tongue, a great thirst, and a love of money. For carrying the news of the Saratoga victory to Congress, he was rewarded with the rank of brigadier general. *DAB*, XX, 222–226.

32. Kingston, then also known as Esopus, was burned by the British on October 16, 1777, as part of General Henry Clinton's efforts at relieving Burgoyne at Saratoga. Hoffman Nickerson, *The Turning Point of the Revolution; or, Burgoyne in America* (Boston and New York, 1928), II, 480; also see George Clinton to Israel Putnam, October 17, 1777: "Kingston was burnt yesterday afternoon because I had not troops to defend it." New York State, *Journals of the Provincial Congress*, I, 1072.

33. According to Heitman, Captain Zachariah Beale of New Hampshire died on October 27, 1777 of wounds received while defending Fort Mercer in Red Bank, New Jersey against a Hessian attack on October 22. Philip claimed that Beale fell as a result of a gunshot wound inflicted by an American sergeant during a rebellion of the New Hampshire troops at Fishkill, New York. The American encampment was described by Thomas Anbury as "a miserable shelter from the severe weather in this country, and I should imagine, must render their troops very sickly, for these huts consist only of little walls made with uneven stones, and the intervals filled up with wood and straw, a few planks forming the roof; there is a chimney at one end, at the side of which is the door." Heitman, p. 93; James H. Smith, *History of Duchess County, New York* (Syracuse, 1882), p. 138.

34. Major Joseph Morris of the First New Jersey Regiment died in January, 1778 of wounds received at Whitemarsh on December 5, 1777. General William Howe had led an attack against Washington's forces as they were marching toward Valley Forge. The Americans held their lines and Howe returned to his main quarters in Philadelphia. Heitman, p. 403; Boatner, pp. 1199–2000.

35. The suffering of the Continental Army at Valley Forge has been depicted countless times by writers and artists. Philip's letters from Valley Forge to General George Clinton and to his father portray the hardships endured as well as the sense of camaraderie which developed at that site. Philip must have been disappointed in not being able to join the main army in their triumphal entry into Philadelphia upon General Henry Clinton's withdrawal. After France became allied with the United States, the British ministry revised their original war plans. As a result, Clinton was compelled to consolidate his forces at New York and relinquish control of Philadelphia to Washington's forces. Washington had other plans for Philip during that time. An entry on June 1, 1778, in the Assistant Deputy Quarter-Master General's *Orderly Book* reads: "Col. Courtland is appoind to tarry in Camp to Superentend the sick left on the Ground when the Army Moves and to Send on the Recoverd men properly Officerd to Join their Respective Corps." Christopher Meng, "Orderly Book containing general orders issued by General Washington at Valley Forge and on the march through Monmouth, N.J. to White Plains, N.Y.," NYPL.

36. When Washington learned that the British under General Henry Clinton were intending to evacuate Philadelphia and march overland to New York in June, 1778, he urged his staff officers to decide on a plan of action. After a good deal of hesitation, it was agreed that the American army was to block the British force at Monmouth, New Jersey. The struggle at Monmouth ensued on June 28 with the Americans retreating at first under General Charles Lee, and then regaining their positions under Washington's personal leadership. Christopher Ward has declared that "Monmouth might be claimed as a victory by both sides with equal justice. Both sides occupied the field, which is the usual criterion of victory. Clinton did not want the

84

field; he wanted to get to New York, which he did. The Americans had repulsed all the attacks on their main position, but that was only a matter of defense, while their real intention was offensive." Ward, II, 576–585.

37. One of the immediate results of the treaty of alliance with France was the appearance of a French naval force off Sandy Hook in July, 1778. Washington determined to use the French fleet in combination with a land force under the command of John Sullivan to free Newport, Rhode Island from British control. Lafayette was to serve under Sullivan during that campaign. The Americans were disappointed in this affair because they did not get the full support of the French force. In fact, primarily because Lieutenant General Comte d'Estaing felt that he had been militarily slighted by Major General Sullivan, did the French commander remove his forces from the conflict on July 21. The American attack then collapsed. Ward, II, 587–592.

38. George Washington informed Congress on November 6, 1778, that he had ordered "Colonel Cortland to march with his regiment towards the MINISINKS and to take such Post as the Governor George Clinton may point out." With this order, Philip and the Second New York Regiment were to become an integral part of the so-called Sullivan-Clinton Campaign.

   Western New York and Pennsylvania were dominated by the warriors of the Six Nations, that is, the confederation of Indians usually referred to as the Iroquois. Philip's letters during the all-out effort to crush the Indians, vividly portrays the savagery pursued by all parties to the conflict.

   Philip's chief adversary was the Mohawk, Joseph Brant, who combined his forces with those of the Loyalist, John Butler, to attack the frontier settlements of New York and Pennsylvania. Although he opposed Brant during the war, Philip hung a portrait of him in his home at Croton after the war Fitzpatrick, XIII, 210; see Philip's letters from Rochester, Jacobs Plains, and Tioga, pp. 132–145.

39. Washington wrote to Philip Van Cortlandt on April 19, 1779 that he was "to move immediately down with your Regiment also [to join Colonel William Malcom] & assist him in the Execution of the Work." This was to consist of opening a road from Easton, Pennsylvania across the Wyoming Territory which stretched across western New York and Pennsylvania. George Washington Papers. LC, Series 3B, reel 19.

40. John Cantine served as a colonel in the Ulster County Militia. *N.Y. in Rev.*, p. 543.

41. Philip Van Cortlandt was with Major General John Sullivan's expedition against the Iroquois in the Wyoming Valley of the Susquehanna River from June 23 to July 31, 1779. The purpose of the expedition was to stop the frontier raids launched from Canada by Tory and Indian forces.

   The immediate task confronting Philip and his men was to clear a road from Easton through the Wyoming Territory, a distance of some sixty-five miles. He completed his portion of the road in thirty days. The difficulty of this project was recognized by General Sullivan when he thanked Philip and Colonel Oliver Spencer of the Fifth New Jersey Regiment for their "unparalleled exertions in clearing and repairing the road to Wyoming." Frederick Cook, ed. *Journals of the Military Expedition of Major General John Sullivan* 1779 (Ann Arbor, Mich., reprint of 1887 ed.) pp. 117–118.

42. According to Heitman, Thomas Boyd of the First Pennsylvania was killed by the Indians on September 13, 1779. Heitman, p. 114.

86

43. This is the third time that Philip became directly embroiled with Benedict Arnold. The two earlier incidents were minor compared to those charges leveled against Arnold stemming from his military command at Philadelphia following General Clinton's evacuation of that city in June 1778. The Council of Pennsylvania had accused Arnold of committing eight violations while supervising the city. A congressional committee determined that some of the charges should be dismissed, others could only be tried in a civil court, and the remainder were subject to review by a court-martial. After a number of delays, the court finally convened at Morristown on December 23, 1779. According to Philip's *Memoir*, a minority sought to have Arnold cashiered out of the army but, instead, he was to be reprimanded by the Commander-in-Chief. It is now known that Arnold was quilty of some of the charges relating to war profiteering, but that a poor case was made against him by the Pennsylvania authorities. Willard M. Wallace, *Traitorous Hero: The Life and Fortunes of Benedict Arnold* (New York, 1954), pp. 180–190; United States Army, *Proceedings Of A General Court Martial For The Trial of Major General Arnold* (New York, 1865), pp. iv-xxix; 1–9; 144–145.

One of the most romanticized figures of the Revolution was the handsome John André, who served as the British secret agent charged with the negotiations concerning Benedict Arnold's turning over the plans of West Point. Hanged as a spy, he became a war legend and highly romanticized accounts of his life and tragic death appeared in the United States. Some examples are: Joshua Hett Smith, *An Authentic Narrative Of The Causes Which Led To The Death Of Major André, Adjutant-General Of His Majesty's Forces In North-America: To which is added A Monody On The Death Of Major André By Miss Seward* (New York, 1809); Egbert Benson, *Vindication Of The Captors Of Major André* (New York, 1817 and 1865);

Winthrop Sargent, *The Life And Career Of Major John André, Adjutant-General Of The British Army In America* (Boston, 1861), 3 vols.

44. The officers mentioned by Philip are:

Seth Warner of New Hampshire had been appointed as a colonel of one of the Sixteen Additional Continental Regiments in July, 1776. Heitman, p. 569.

Walter Stewart of Pennsylvania served in the Thirteenth Pennsylvania Regiment. *Ibid.*, pp. 520–521.

Matthias Ogden was taken prisoner at Elizabethtown, New Jersey on October 5, 1780. *Ibid.*, p. 418.

William Shepherd or Shepard of Massachusetts was connected to the Fourth Massachusetts Regiment. *Ibid.*, p. 493.

Herman Swift of Connecticut bore the rank of colonel throughout the war. He was breveted as a brigadier general in September, 1783. *Ibid.*, p. 530.

Colonel Jean-Joseph Sourbader de Gimat distinguished himself during the siege of Yorktown. Howard C. Rice, Jr. and Anne S. K. Brown, eds. *The American Campaigns of Rochambeau's Army* 1780, 1781, 1782, 1783 (Princeton, 1972), I, 149.

"Light-Horse Harry" Lee of Revolutionary War fame authored the *Memoirs of the War in the Southern Department of the United States*, published in 1812. In July, 1779 he surprised the British at Powles Hook in New Jersey in what has been characterized as "one of the most brilliant feats of the war." *DAB*, XI, pp. 107–108.

The "Majors Command of Artilery" was under the direction of William Macpherson. He served as an aide to General Benjamin Lincoln to the end of the war. Fitzpatrick, XIX, 299.

45. By an act of Congress adopted in September, 1780, the divisions of the Continental Line were reorganized. Under

88

the new arrangement, New York was to have two infantry regiments and one of artillery. The infantry regiments were to "consist of nine companies," with each company comprised of "64 non-commissioned officers & privates." *Papers of George Clinton*, VI, 279.

46. Lieutenant Colonel Robert Cochran of the Second New York, had previously served as a captain in a Connecticut company under Benedict Arnold. In May, 1779 Cochran wrote to George Clinton seeking four hundred acres at Crown Point. His petition contains an outline of his services to that date. [New York State], *Calendar of Historical Manuscripts, Relating to the War of the Revolution, in the Office of the Secretary of State, Albany, N.Y.* (Albany, 1868), II, 335–336.

47. Jean-Louis-Ambroise de Genton, chevalier de Villefranche began his career in the Continental Army as a captain of engineers and rose in rank to that of a lieutenant colonel. Several of his maps are still extant. Rice and Brown, *American Campaigns of Rochambeau's Army*, I, 345.

48. Peter Elsworth served in a militia company commanded by Marinus Willett. Fernow, p. 258.

49. Captain Andrew Moodie of the Second Continental Artillery received his commission in January, 1777. Heitman, p. 397.

50. Washington's forces in the north, as of May-June 1781, were at a sad stage. Washington wrote in his journal, "Instead of having the prospect of a glorious offensive campaign before us, we have a bewildered and gloomy defensive one, unless we receive a powerful aid of ships, land troops and money from our general allies." That help came in the form of the French General Jean-Baptiste-

Donatien de Vimeur, comte de Rochambeau with infantry, artillery and cavalry. With these added forces, Washington contemplated attacking New York City. Upon thoroughly reconnoitering the British forces on Manhattan Island, Washington and his commanding officers determined to abandon the plan and turn their attention instead to Cornwallis' army in the southern theater. Ward, II, 880–881.

51. Late in July, 1781 General Washington informed Major General Alexander McDougall that he was ordering Van Cortlandt's regiment to the vicinity of West Point, and that "as soon as it arrives you will be pleased to send that and the light Company of Van Schaicks to join the Army." Washington to Alexander McDougall, July 27, 1781 in Fitzpatrick, XXII, p. 421.

52. The purpose of this maneuvering was to keep General Henry Clinton and the British army in New York from suspecting the true destination of Washington's forces. The American movement was to appear as preparations for another effort at attacking New York City. Clinton did not become aware of Washington's true intentions until September 2, at which time the American forces had already reached Philadelphia on their march southward. *Ibid.*, pp. 882–883.

Washington wrote Major General Benjamin Lincoln on August 24, 1781 that "The Detachments under your Command is to march to Springfield in New Jersey, by two Routs; the left Column with which you will go, is to be compos'd of the light troops, and York Regiments (if Courtlands should get to you in time)." *Ibid.*, XXIII, 41.

Then on the next day he issued the following orders to Philip Van Cortlandt:

"You will take charge of the Clothing, the Boats, Intrenching Tools, and such other Stores as shall be committed to your care by the Quarter Master General: With these you are to proceed (in the Order they are mentioned) to Springfield, by the way of Suffern's Pompton, the two Bridges and Chatham.

"When you arrive at Springfield you will put yourself under the Orders of Maj^r. Gen^r. Lincoln, or any other your sen^r. Officer commandg. at that place. (You will also, of occassion should require it alter the above Route agreeably to Orders from either Major Genl. Lincoln or the Quarter M. Genl.

You will be particularly careful to collect all your Men that are in a proper condition to march and will use your best endeavores to prevent desertion." George Washington Papers, LC, Series 4, reel 80.

53. Abraham Lott and Lucas Beaverhout owned farms which lay near the intersection of the Parsippany turnpike and the road between Troy Hills and Lower Montville. Ambrose E. VanDerpoel, *Chatham, New Jersey* (Chatham, 1959), p. 324.

54. Marie-Joseph-Paul-Roch-Yves-Gilbert de Motier, marquis de Lafayette arrived in America on April 20, 1777. He soon became a volunteer on Washington's staff and was given a command of his own in December. He saw action several times during the following year, and journeyed to France in January 1779. He returned in April 1780 and joined the talks between Washington and Rochambeau. Lafayette soon was active in the Southern campaign and was, of course, in the midst of the fighting at Yorktown. Philip and Lafayette struck up a lasting friendship and the two warriors were reunited in 1824 when the Frenchman again came to New York. *DAB*, X, 536–538.

The Colonel Hamilton mentioned here is the famous Alexander Hamilton. The Van Cortlandt family remained

NOTES

on close terms with Hamilton after the war and used his legal services on many occasions until the time of his death. Collections of Sleepy Hollow Restorations.

55. Major Nicholas Fish of the Second New York was commissioned on November 21, 1776. He served until the end of the conflict. Heitman, p. 227.

56. Alexander Scammell of New Hampshire had served together with Philip at Saratoga. He was an outstanding officer who, while on a mission at Yorktown, was shot by one of Tarleton's men allegedly after he had surrendered. Ward, II, 506, 888–889.

57. Some 8,845 Americans and 7,800 Frenchmen converged on Cornwallis' army of six thousand men at Yorktown on September 28, 1781. One day later, Cornwallis withdrew his troops from the outlying redoubts, with the exception of the so-called Fusiliers' Redoubt, and regrouped them within Yorktown. In the effort to take the Fusiliers' Redoubt on September 30, Colonel Scammell was captured and killed.

The siege of Yorktown lasted until October 16, by which time Cornwallis realized that his situation was hopeless. Washington asked for and received an unconditional surrender and the formalities of its acceptance occurred on the 19th. The Americans captured 7,247 soldiers and eight hundred and forty sailors, resulting in the close of the war in the South. Ward, II, 886–895; John R. Alden, *The South in the Revolution 1763–1789* (*A History of the South*, III, Baton Rouge, La., 1957), pp. 295–298.

58. Antoine-Charles du Houx, baron de Vioménil was second in command of Rochambeau's army. Rice and Brown, *American Campaigns of Rochambeau's Army*, I, 11; 334.

59. George Baylor of Virginia commanded a famous group of cavalrymen from his home state. During a skirmish at Old Tappan in Rockland County, New York in September, 1778, British General Charles Grey surprised Baylor and his men while they were asleep in several barns. Thirty-six men were bayoneted, and Major Baylor was wounded and captured. Ward, II, 616–617.

60. Introduced by Benjamin Franklin as "a Lieutenant General in the King of Prussia's service," Friedrich Wilhelm Augustus von Steuben came to America in December 1777. He had served as a staff member under Frederick the Great during the Seven Years' War, but had not risen above the rank of captain. His chief claim to fame was his great success in creating a well-trained army at Valley Forge in the winter and spring of 1778. He was elevated to Major General Inspector General in May 1778. Boatner, pp. 1055–1058.

61. Captain Henry Vanderburgh transferred to the Second New York Regiment in January, 1781. Heitman, p. 555.

62. Benjamin Lincoln accepted terms by which his American army was to be considered as prisoners of war, while the militiamen were allowed to return to their homes as prisoners on parole. Ward, II, 703.

63. Elias Dayton of the Third New Jersey was promoted to Brigadier General of the Continental Army in January, 1783. Heitman, p. 190.

64. The Baptist minister John Gano (1727–1804), of New Rochelle, New York, became a chaplain for the New York forces of the Continental line. He served in the Sullivan-Clinton Campaign on the western frontier and accompanied the New York regiments on many of their expedi-

tions. He later became a regent of the University of the State of New York and a trustee of Columbia College. *DAB*, VII, 125.

65. George and Martha Washington left Morristown, New Jersey on the morning of March 28 and stopped at the "York Hutts" near Pompton on the 30th. Fitzpatrick, XXIV, 94; William S. Baker, *Itinerary of General Washington from June* 15, 1775 *to December* 23, 1783 (Philadelphia, 1892), p. 259.

66. Philip is referring to the so-called "Newburgh Conspiracy," which is still a matter of much historical dispute. It is now accepted that the author of the anonymous Address was John Armstrong, Jr., who warned the Army officers that if they did not take bold action immediately in order to obtain some redress of their grievances, "every future effort is in vain; and your threats then, will be as empty as your entreaties now." It is of historical importance to note that Philip mentions a meeting he attended along with other brigade commanders called at the instigation of George Washington at which all agreed to support Washington. This meeting occurred prior to the famous gathering of the officers in the "New Building" on Saturday morning, March 15, 1783. For a discussion of the events surrounding this affair see: Richard H. Kohn, "The Inside History of the Newburgh Conspiracy: America and the Coup d'Etat, *The William and Mary Quarterly*, 3rd. Ser. (April 1970), XXVII, No. 2, 187–220; Paul D. Nelson, "Horatio Gates at Newburgh, 1783: A Misunderstood Role," with a "Rebuttal" by Richard Kohn in *Ibid.*, XXIX (January 1972), 143–148; C. Edward Skeen, "The Newburgh Conspiracy Reconsidered," with a "Rebuttal" by Richard H. Kohn in *Ibid.*, XXXI (April 1974), 273–298.

67. The Society of the Cincinnati was created by the Continental Army officers in May 1783 as a "Society of Friends, to endure so long as they shall endure, or any of their eldest male posterity. . . . " Washington accepted the presidency of the organization in June. Philip remained active in the New York division throughout the remainder of his life. Boatner, pp. 229–230; Society of Cincinnati Papers, NYHS.

68. Philip wrote to Governor George Clinton on June 5, 1783 that "the officers of the Second New York Regiment (in Testimony of their attachment and Esteem) intend doing themselves the honor of presenting your Excellency with their Regimental Standard Colours and instruments of Musick . . . ."

Clinton answered, "I shall be happy in waiting upon them [officers of the Second New York] at my home on Saturday next and the Pleasure of their Company at Dinner on that Day . . . ." *Papers of George Clinton*, VIII, 193–194.

69. Lieutenant William Colbreath was the Quarter Master for the Second New York from January, 1781 until June, 1783. *Ibid*; Heitman, p. 163.

70. John Francis Hamtramck was a career officer who remained in the Army at the conclusion of the Revolution. He rose to the rank of colonel in 1802. Heitman, p. 271.

Henry Vanderburgh served in the Second New York under Philip. *Ibid.*, p. 555.

"Dr. Pryer" was most likely Abner William Pryor who served as a Surgeon's Mate in the Fourth New York. *N.Y. in Rev.*, p. 209.

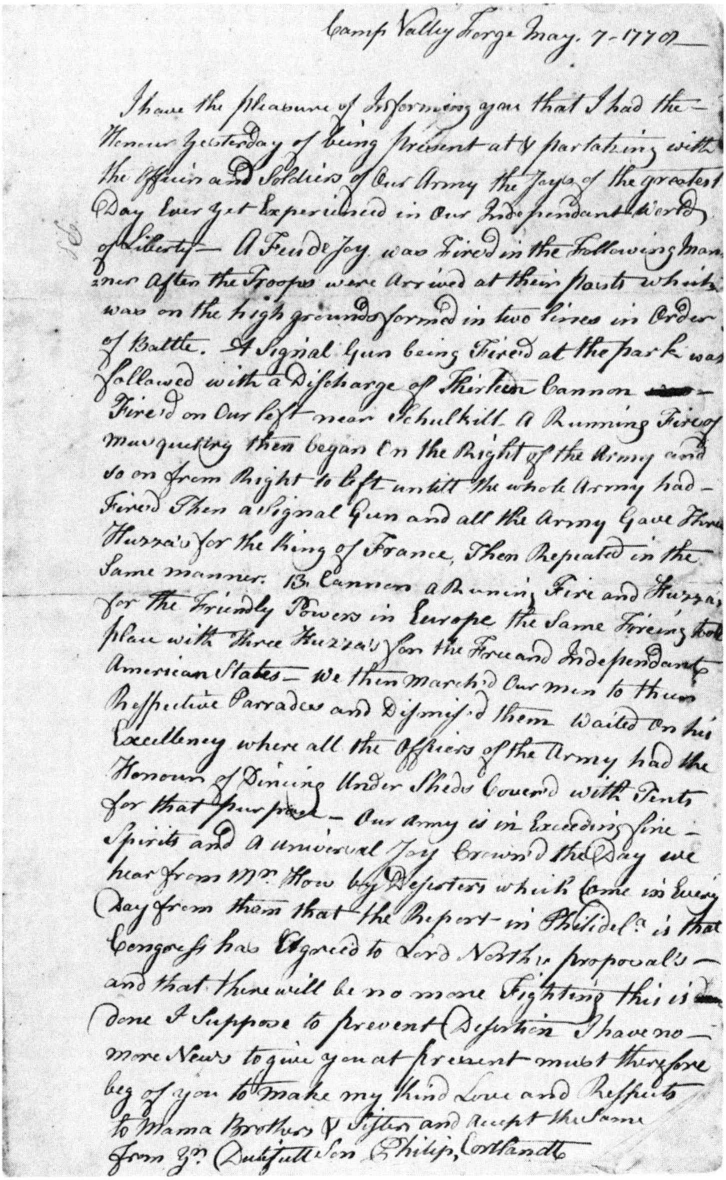

Camp Valley Forge May. 7-1778—

I have the pleasure of Informing you that I had the Honour Yesterday of being present at & partaking with the Officers and Soldiers of Our Army the Joys of the greatest Day Ever yet Experienced in Our Independant World of Liberty— A Feu de Joy was Fired in the Following Manner After the Troops were Arrived at their Posts which was on the high grounds formed in two Lines in Order of Battle. A Signal Gun being Fired at the park was followed with a Discharge of Thirteen Cannon Fired on Our left near Schulkill A Running Fire of Musquetry then began On the Right of the Army and so on from Right to left untill the whole Army had Fired Then a Signal Gun and all the Army Gave Three Huzza's for the King of France, Then Repeated in the Same manner. 13 Cannon a Runing Fire and Huzza's for the Friendly Powers in Europe the Same Fireing took place with Three Huzza's for the Free and Independant American States— We then March'd Our men to their Respective Parrades and Dismiss'd them Waited on his Excellency where all the Officers of the Army had the Honour of Dining Under Sheds Covered with Tents for that Purpose— Our Army is in Exceeding fine Spirits and A Universal Joy Crown'd the Day we hear from Mr. How by Deserters which Come in Every Day from them that the Report in Philidel.a is that Congress has Agreed to Lord North's proposals— and that there will be no more Fighting this is done I Suppose to prevent Desertion I have no more News to give you at present must therefore beg of you to make my kind Love and Respects to Mama Brothers & Sisters and Accept the Same from Yr. Dutifull Son Philip Cortlandt

LETTER

from Philip Van Cortlandt to his Father, datelined at Camp Valley Forge, May 7, 1778. (See pages 124–127). Philip Van Cortlandt describes the military celebration by the Army upon their receiving the glorious news that France had allied herself to the American cause of independence. Courtesy of Manuscripts and Archives Division, The New York Public Library.

Introduction *to*
Selected Correspondence

T HE SELECTED WARTIME CORRESPONDENCE of Philip Van Cortlandt lends additional substance to the events mentioned in his *Memoir*. The letters have been chosen because they either convey further information concerning an important event or provide new information, or because they serve as expositions of his particular attitudes. The years 1777, 1782, and 1783 are not included in this selection because they represent either routine correspondence or repetitive material. The selected letters amply depict, for example, Philip's disillusionment with Congressional treatment of the army units, a topic which is not alluded to in the *Memoir*. Similarly, the shortage of funds which plagued him as an officer of a combat ready unit becomes clear from reading Philip's letters to his father and to John Jay.

Although he regarded himself as having been taught to "write badly" his thoughts are quite apparent to the reader. Philip's times of joy and of dismay are readily evident from his changing attitudes as displayed in these letters.

The correspondence yields a picture of a young man who was placed in an important leadership position at a relatively early age and who then matured while serving in a commanding capacity for over eight years. Never much given to deep philosophical introspection, on occasion Philip lets us view his innermost thoughts and fears. These letters also help us understand the abiding affection which developed between him and his father. This was a reciprocated affection, later demonstrated by the way Pierre addressed his son. The salutation adopted after 1783 by the father in most of his letters to his son read "Dear General."

Philip Van Cortlandt. AD
NYPL

[ca. 1775–1778]

My
Journal of some part of the life of
Mrs. Beekman & Judge Livingston
&c &c
& a part of my Journal
in 1776 & 1777[1]

My Dear Sir,

I have made a short statement of my history in Life & herewith transmit it for your Information—Viz—Ph. V. C. who was born in N. York 1 Sepr. 1749—was brought up at Croton where he now resides—and received most of his Education at an Academy and at the age of 19 Commenced business as a Surveyor, Suprinting [superintending] sales of Lan^d, a Flowring Mill and Country store untill the year 1775 (when he gave up all his persuits of making a fortune) and on the Britt distroying Lexing & Concord—his mind in concord with that of his Patriotick Father was fixed to oppose the Tyranick oppression of British government—not withstanding his Tory Relations wanted him to Join their standard and receive an additional commiss^n from Govr Tryon who had Previously Made me a Major of the Militia in the County of Westchester—But my determination being Liberty or Death I threw Tryons Comm^n in the Fire and Rec^d, Rec^d & L. C. Com^n signed J^o Hancock President of the U.S.—in June 1775. I continued L^t. Col^o. of the 4 N. York untill Novr 1776 —when the Co$^{[l]}$ of the 2^d having Joined the Enemy—Genl. Washing being Provided with blank Com^s. had my name put in Com^n as Col^o. of the 2^d N. Y. Reg^t. and Sent it Lake Champlain where I was in Command at Skeensborough with orders to join his Army under his Com^d marching thro N.J. to the state of Pen^a. but I did not over take the Reg^t. untill the day after the Capture of the Heshins—in the Morning and Saw the Prisoners Cross the River—I was ordered to Recruit the Reg^t. at Fishkill and the Next year 1777 I had the Com of West^r. untill Genl. Washington order'd my Command to Albany and assisted in the capture of Genl. Burgoin's Army who I saw ground their Arms as Prisoners. &c &c after their Disappoint of going thro the Woods unobserved by our army to Albany on the 18th day of Sepr 1777—which might have been affected had not their Intintion been discovered by myself about the break of day when I sent an Express to G[eneral]. Gates to Inform G. Arnold and Col^o. Morgan to proceed Immediately West in the Woods to Interrupt their Intended March which they did but the next day they again made the attempt which brought on the famous Battle of the 19th of Sep^r.

After the Capture of Burgoyns Army I was with my

100

Command order'd to Join Genl. Washington in the State of Pennsylvania which did and after Cantooning my Reg^t. in Huts—the Genl. sent me with a Command in fort Radner 9 miles from P[hiladelphia] & 34 m^s ad^v[ance] of our Army—and after my Result gave me the Command of the encampment at V[alley] F[orge] when he pursued the British army at Munmuth C[ourt] H[ouse].

    After compleating the Genl. Orders at V.F. I join'd my Reg^t at Wh. P[lains] and continued with army untill I

[from margin]
1778

was sent on the Western Frontier of this State to oppose G[eneral] Br[ant] the Indian—where I remain'd all Winter & in the Spring was ordered by Express from G. Washington to Join G. Sullivan going on to subdue the Indians—which duly I perform'd and among other things had the honer of routing their Forces under the s^d G. Brant by Making a charge with Baonit at Newtown

[from margin]
1779

Hill in Tioga tier after my return I join'd G. W. again at Morris Town and made Huts under Genl. Clintons Command.

    In 1780 my command was order to the S—N. Y. and I had a Com^d. of Infantry under G—Lafaette untill Novr. when I was first sent to Albany then to Schenectady then to Fort Stanwix and Remain'd untill General Washing came from Chatham in N.Y.—to deliver his orders to me in person and which I obeyed untill I join Genl. Clinton in Baltimore and proceeded to James River in Virginia and as Genl. Clinton Com^d. the Division of N. Y. & New Jersey troops I com^d. the N. Y. brigade—and had the Lines before York the Morning after our Arrival. Previous to which Col^o. Scammel was killed and Genl. Washington came up to see the lines and gave me Verbal orders to place Centinels at night round York to guard on the Right to York River and ordered Baron Van Ameni^l [Viomenil] to place them on the left—which was done and the British found themselves Surrounded in the Morning as we had Troops at Gloster Point on the north side of the River—

After the Capture as Gen Clinton & Daton went by Water I had the Command of the Division of Y. & J Troops which I march'd by land to the State of N J.——leaving 700 Prisoners at Fredericksburgh. I Hutted the Y. Troops at Pumpton N Jersey. 1781 & 1782.

Judge. Died the 9th Decr. 1775—Montgomery

[from margin]
1775

31—1775 in Decr. I left Ticonderoga in Company of

[from margin]
1776
5 Jany Uncle
   B Died

Genl. Schuyler Jany. I came from Albany on a pair of Scaits & Lay the night at Lonningburgh Next day went to

102

M^rs. Livingstons Dine'd & after Dinner went on Scates to Rhinebeck found Gitty Livingston there.²

[from margin]
Aunt Beekman Died in March
1777

I Rode a Sorrel Horse with a short Tail I had him of Bart Turtle, I slept at Rhinebeck and left it Early and at Johns Town I took the Ancrum Road out of my Way and Came into the Road where Platner³ lives—and stoped in Claverack at 11 Oclock Found M^rs. Montgomery at Genl. Schuylers She & Ann went with me to Fort Edward Left them & went to Ticonderoga. My horse was pastured out—in the summer I rode down Capt. Oharra Horse my servant had—I came to Jacob Thomas⁴ he lent me a pair of horses—which I rode to Kingsbridge to Genl. Washington & returned—late the fall I came Al-

[from margin]
1777

bany & exchanged my horse with Pierre for a black Stallion which I Rode to Pennsylvania & Returned to Fishkill in the Winter went with pierre & Mama to Claverack left Claverack Sunday Evening with Sister Nancy rode in the Night to Genl. Tenbrooks—Next day went to Rhine beck the Old Gentleman came there Next

[from margin]
it [was] at that time I slept in the
S.E. Room

day. Aunt Beekman was then alive—I went to Vissit M^{rs}. Livingston after which I went to Esopus & with Gilbert Livingston.

NOTES

1. After reading Philip's *Memoir* it becomes easier to follow this abbreviated outline of his wartime activities. Whether this was prepared prior to the *Memoir* or as a result of it cannot be readily ascertained. Its sudden breaking off in 1782 leaves one to conclude that at least another page existed at an earlier time. The title, furthermore, suggests that this was part of a more ambitious project which either remained incomplete or has been lost. It is my personal belief that it was written prior to the *Memoir*, since he varied his tenses and pronouns in an uncoordinated manner, whereas in the *Memoir* Philip never referred to himself in the artificial third person singular.

    This version does contain information not included in the *Memoir*. For example, here he states, "and at the age of 19 Commenced business as a Surveyor." This definite age is not mentioned in the *Memoir*. He also pinpoints the time when he and his father determined to adhere to the cause of independence when he asserts: "and on the Britt[ish] distroying Lexing[ton] & Concord—his mind in concord with that of his Patriotick Father was fixed to oppose the Tyranick oppression of British government." This is somewhat at variance with the *Memoir*, which emphasizes Governor Tryon's visit to Van Cortlandt Manor early in 1774.

    Perhaps a more complete manuscript did include a "Journal of some part of the life of Mrs. Beekman & Judge Livingston," but the references to them here are minimal.

    His statement concerning the horses used during the early part of the war is not found in any other document and, therefore, is of some interest.

2. Judge Robert R. Livingston (August 1718–December 9, 1775) had served as a judge of the New York Supreme Court, as a member of the Committee of Correspondence,

and as a New York representative to the Stamp Act Congress. Philip's mother was a Livingston.

The cryptic "Montgomery 31 — 1775" refers to the death of General Richard Montgomery during the attack on Quebec on December 31, 1775. Montgomery was married to Janet Livingston, daughter of Judge Robert R. Livingston. These allusions and the marginal notations relating to the death of his great-aunt and great-uncle, Henry and Gertrude Beekman, are probably associated with Van Cortlandt claims to Livingston estate rights.

Philip obviously skated down the Hudson from General Philip Schuyler's home in Albany to Loonenburgh (later called Athens) on the west bank of the Hudson River opposite Claverack Landing (now Hudson). From there he continued to the home of his mother's relations in Rhincbeck by crossing the Hudson again on skates. Cuyler Reynolds, *Genealogical and Family History of Southern New York and the Hudson River Valley* (New York, 1914), III, 1336–1337; *DAB*, XIII, 320–321; See Genealogy, pp. 19–23.

3. Ancram was a small community within the Livingston Patent in Columbia County. Iron had been mined there since the 1750s. Jacob Platner was listed in the First Federal Census of 1790 as a head of household residing in Columbia County. French, pp. 242–243; Genealogical Publishing Company, *Heads of Families At The First Census Of The United States Taken In The Year 1790: New York* (Baltimore, 1971), p. 71.

4. Jacob Thomas was a resident of the Town of Cortlandt and his family consisted of a wife, a son, and four daughters. *Ibid.*, p. 197.

⚜ 2 ⚜

Philip to [Unknown][1]
New York State, *Journals of the Provincial Congress,
Provincial Convention, Committee of Safety of the State of New
York,* 1775–1777 (Albany, 1842), I, 137–138.

Albany, August 28, 1775

DEAR SIR: Agreeable to verbal orders received from Colonel Holmes,[2] when last in New-York, made all the despatch in my power to this place, where I arrived the 26th instant. Finding Captain Henry B. Livingston,[3] with his Company, in a small house in Town, he wants many things, such as shoes, shirts, stockings, underclothes, haversacks, and cash, having advanced all himself that has been paid his men as yet.

The day I arrived came up the following Captains, with their Companies: Captain Herrick, Captain Palmer, Captain Hertell, and Captain Mills, all without blankets, except Captain David Palmer;[4] many of the men wanting shirts, shoes, stockings, underclothes, and, in short, without any thing fit for a soldier except a uniform coat, and not more than thirty guns, with four Companies, fit for service. They are now on board the small boats that brought them up, having no place for them to go into, as there is not one tent that I can find for our Battalion, and three Companies without blankets, and none to be had at this place. I do not know how to act, or what to do with them: they begin to ask for cash and better lodgings, being much crowded in the small boats in which I am

107

obliged to keep them. I this morning made application to the Committee of Albany, who will do all in their power for me, which I believe is but very little. Shall be much obliged to the honourable Congress to send me with all convenient speed arms, blankets, tents, shoes, stockings, haversacks, and cash, by all means. I want to be going forward, where, by what I can learn, we shall be wanting if we can go soon, or not at all. The men say, give us guns, blankets, tents, &c., and we will fight the devil himself; but do not keep us here in market boats, as though we were a parcel of sheep or calves. In short, nothing can give me more pleasure than the arrival of the aforesaid articles; until which, shall do all in my power to keep the men together, and in as good order as clubs and canes can keep them, without arms to keep a proper guard; as I have orders from the General to collect all the arms together and send as many men off directly to Ticonderoga,[5] (and that without tents,) which will not be a full Company unless I can purchase some arms here.

I remain, dear Sir, your most obedient
humble servant,

PHILIP CORTLANDT,
Lt. Col. of the Fourth Battalion.

P.S. The cash I received I was obliged to pay to the mutinous men in the lower barracks,[6] and I sent by Lieut. Riker, to Captain Woodard, at New-Town, Long-Island, some part of it.

1. Philip apparently sent this letter to an individual, who, in turn submitted it to the Albany Committee of Safety. That committee then sent a cover letter to the New York Provincial Congress in which they stated:

> We expected when the army was once organized, we should not be so frequently called upon about matters not in our province. But the situation of Col. Van Cortlandt and the men under his command, in a great measure obliges us to give him all the assistance in our power—not, however, that it is to be made a precedent of. The enclosed letter from Col. Van Cortlandt will show you the posture he is in, and the necessity of a speedy relief. We feel we shall be able to afford him but little assistance.
>
> New York State, *Journals of the Provincial Congress, Provincial Convention, Committee of Safety and Council of Safety of the State of New York* 1775–1777 (Albany, 1842), I, 137–138.

2. James Holmes of Westchester County was commissioned as the colonel of the Fourth New York Regiment in June 1775. He later joined the Loyalists. *D. Col. N.Y.*, XV, 252.

3. Henry B. Livingston was the son of William Livingston who served as New Jersey's first governor. Henry entered the service in November 1776 and resigned as a colonel in January 1779. He acted as John Jay's secretary during the latter's service as minister to Spain, 1779–1782. *Ibid*, p. 209; *DAB*, XI, 312–313.

4. Captain Rufus Herrick served in the Fourth New York Regiment, *D. Col. N.Y.*, XV, 17, 253: Captain David Palmer

commanded the Richmond County Company of the Fourth Regiment, *ibid*., p. 529: Daniel Mills commanded a Westchester County Company in the Fourth Regiment: Hertell was possibly Abraham Hartwell. An Abraham Hartwell served as captain of a Dutchess County Militia Company. *N.Y. in Rev.* p. 279.

5. The so-called "Gibraltar of America," Fort Ticonderoga was captured by Ethan Allen and Benedict Arnold on May 10, 1775. It fell to the British forces in July 1777. On August 29, 1775, Colonel Goose Van Schaick notified the New York Provincial Congress that he had arrived in Albany following General Philip Schuyler's order to forward the troops to Ticonderoga. He reported that "Col⁰ Van Cortlandt is also arrived here with 5 Companies of Holmes' Battalion, who have not arms sufficient to supply 1 Company." Boatner, pp. 1100–1103; *N.Y. in Rev*., p. 36.

6. Van Schaick also stated that "the men are much discontented for want of their pay, & do accuse you, that the service greatly suffers. There is scarce anything to be heard in the Camp but Mutinies." *Ibid*.

◦⊰{ 3 }⊱◦

Philip to Philip Schuyler. ALS
NYPL

Albany May 28th 1776

D.ʳ General

    Agreeable to Your Orders[1] Rec.ᵈ have Sent 25 Men of Capt. OHarra's Comp.ʸ under the Command of Lieu.ᵗ Abiel Sherewood[2] to half moon to gaurd the provisions at that place[3] Cap.ᵗ Sam.ˡ Van Veghton with his Company marched Yesterday for Fort George[4] Lieu.ᵗ Beeker of Cap.ᵗ V. Sanfoords's Comp.ʸ Marched at Same time to M.ʳ Learn's Mill with Orders to gaurd the provisions with about 12 Men being all he had with him—[5]

    Cap.ᵗ OHarra & the Remainder of his Company being about   Men I have order'd to StillWater[6] my Reasons for Sending him are first Cap.ᵗ Veeder is not as yet Supply'd with any thing but guns having no Kittles nor None to be had 2.ᵈˡʸ all the Forces are Order'd from this place Except my men which are only Cap.ᵗ Vossburg and Cap.ᵗ Veeder to man the Batteaus and Keep a Quarter Guard at this place which is Highly Necessary as there is Several prisoners to be Tryed In the Guard House Hope the General will not Take it amiss as Absolute Necessaty Obliges me to keep some Orderly men here which Cap.ᵗ Veeders Comp.ʸ Meritts and is more than I can say of Cap.ᵗ OHarra's the Cap.ᵗ I think will be better

111

able to govern his men at Fresh Still Water than here where Strong Waters are to be had—I have Sent M[r] Thomas Williams Quarter Master[8] to New York with Orders for all Such Stores Allow'd by Congress for Our Reg[t]—Cap[t] Jacob W. Seeber[9] has been with me I let him have Three Hundred pounds two of which I borrow'd of the pay Master[10] on Acc[t] for him which is not Sufficient to pay his Billet to the first of may his Comp[y] is full but wants Every thing almost no Guns nor any to be had in that County as he Says. M[r] Renslaer[11] has bought them up the other Comp[y] in Tryon County is in the Same Situation

Shall be Exceeding glad to know the Generals pleasure I think it will be best to Order them to this place to be got in Order and are much wanting besides as they have no arms nor likely to get any they can be of Very little Use Where they are Unless they Fight with Wooden Guns which the Cap[t] Says they have made to Excersise with—Waiting Your Further Commands Am With Great Respect

Your Ob[t] and Very
Hum[l] Ser[t]
Philip Cortlandt Lieu[t] Col[o]

---

1. Philip Schuyler was in command of the Northern Army. After the Americans had been routed in the disastrous Canadian invasion, Schuyler had to secure the safety of the retreating forces. Philip Van Cortlandt was placed in charge of a number of bateaus. After being used for the purposes of transporting his men and supplies, they were to be returned to Fort George with men from the Canada campaign. *Philip Schuyler to Charles Don, May 30, 1776,* NYPL.

2. Henry O'Hara recruited a line company consisting of himself as captain, an ensign, two sergeants, four corporals, a drummer and fifer along with thirty-seven privates as of May 10. He assured the Provincial Congress that he would soon recruit more men in Albany and Charlotte Counties, the region encompassing Lake Champlain and what is now Vermont. *N.Y. in Rev.*, p. 101. Abiel or Adiel Sherwood was then serving as a first lieutenant in the First N.Y. Regiment. *Ibid.*, pp. 139, 181.

3. An important Hudson River ferry crossing existed at Half Moon Point, now known as Waterford. French, p. 593.

4. Samuel Van Veghten served in the First New York Regiment. Fort George was located at the southern end of Lake George. *N.Y. in Rev.*, p. 180; Boatner, pp. 389–390.

5. Lieutenant Beeker or Becker and Captain Cornelius Van Santvoord or Santvoort served in Col. Cornelius Wynkoop's Regiment in 1776. *Cal. H. Mss.*, II, 44.

6. Stillwater was the site of one of the major battles between Generals Gates and Burgoyne in September 1777. Benson J. Lossing, *Pictorial Field-Book of the Revolution* (New York, 1850), II, 51–52.

7. Abraham Veeder and an Isaac P. Vosburgh were captains in the New York Militia. *N.Y. in the Rev.*, pp. 266–268.

8. Thomas T. Williams, Jr., was recommended in March 1776 as the Quartermaster of the New York Regiment to be raised in Albany, Tryon, and Charlotte Counties. *Ibid.*, p. 85.

9. Jacob W. Seeber served in a Tryon County Levy Battalion. *Ibid.*, p. 294.

10. The pay master for Van Cortlandt's regiment was Robert Provoost. *Ibid.*, p. 186.

11. Most likely Philip was referring to Kilian Van Rensselaer, Colonel of an Albany County Regiment. *Ibid.*, p. 264.

⊷⧼ 4 ⧽⊷

Philip to New York Provincial Congress
NY Provincial Congress, II, 287–288.

Ticonderoga, Augt 5, 1776

GENTLEMEN—This acknowledges the receipt of a letter from Mr. John McKesson,[1] dated N.Y. July 14th, last,
relative to Colo. Wynkoop's regiment.[2] When I was at
Albany had not time to procure the dates of all the
officers' warrants; the Committee promised to have the
matter settled. I have paid the billet of six companies; the
two raised in Tryon county have not settled with, but
borrowed money on account, of the paymaster for them;
shortly after which I was ordered to this place by General
Schuyler, since which have not had it in my power to
make a return, the regiment being in such a divided
state, but shall make out one as soon as possible. I
have enclosed your letter to Colo. Wynkoop, who is at
Skeensburgh.

Permit me, gentlemen, by this opportunity, to
transmit to you a few observations on my present situation, being confident that nothing is wanting on your
part to promote the welfare of the United States, or to do
justice to those who have risked their all for its defence.
Many of you, gentlemen, I have the honour to be per-
sonally acquainted with, which emboldens me to appeal
to you for my character in private life; for my behaviour

115

as an officer, the generals under whom I served the preceding and present campaigns can testify. It was not for ease, or to have an exalted commission that brought me to the field. On the contrary, numbers of you, gentlemen, I flatter myself, know that I lived in affluence at home, and consequently, that I was not induced into the service with a view to the pay, as you must all be satisfied; that it is not an object for a gentleman. When that respectable Body, with which I had the honour of serving in representing this State, offered me a commission from the Continental Congress, last summer, I with reluctance accepted, not from a want of zeal to do my injured country all the service I was capable of, but a diffidence in my own mind of my abilities to fill such an important office as that of lieut. colonel of a regiment. I am at present the first lieut. colonel in this army, as I am informed, and I believe may safely add, in the service of the United States. Notwithstanding, must, to do my country justice, and not myself, bear the mortification to see several officers promoted to the command of regiments in the Continental army which I commanded last campaign. Justice to those gentlemen of our State who entered into the service and have undergone the fatigue of last winter's campaign in Canada, superior in rank, and who have been distinguished throughout the army for their bravery and honour, are also superseded by the late appointments of officers for Colo. Duboys's regiment, &c. This must be evident, when the rank roll of last year is examined into for the character of the officers. I can not conclude without suggesting to you that I was by an ill state of health, prevented from going into Canada, and there joining the army then in that quarter. My honour as a gentleman, I conceive hurt and injured by being thus neglected and superseded, and lest you might think that I was ignorant thereof, I have taken this method of informing you of it; but the same principles of honour which tells me that I am disregarded, assures me also that it would be most shameful for me to resign at present, when the enemy of the States have attacked the State of which I am a citizen, at both extremities. I must, however, observe to you, that I shall be obliged in justice to myself, to resign my commission after the cloud which now hangs over us in this part is dispelled; and I shall do it with the more cheerfulness, as I conceive it will be agreeable to those from whom I have received it, or they would not have given me the private intimation by superseding.

Be assured, gentlemen, however, that if ever it lies in my power to render any service to my country, or to the cause of liberty and mankind, no man will be more ready in doing it.

I have the honour to be, gent. with respect,
Your most obt. and very humble servant,
PHILIP CORTLANDT.

[Addressed]
To the President and gentlemen convened,
representing the State of New-York.

---

1. John McKesson was Secretary to the New York Council of Safety and a few days prior to this letter had been appointed as Register in Chancery by the Provincial Convention. *Papers of George Clinton*, I, 196–197.

2. Under the most recent rearrangement of New York troops, Cornelius D. Wynkoop was designated as colonel of a regiment in which Philip was second in command. Force, *Archives*, *V*, I, 919. Meanwhile, Congress was preparing to promote and reorganize the Continental forces. Edward Rutledge wrote to Robert R. Livingston in August 1776,

> It will give me real pleasure I assure you to do justice to Mr. Courtland and promote your brother [Henry Beekman Livingston] to the rank, which his services and situation in my opinion demand. . . . I think there should be no difficulty in giving Lt Col. Courtland McDougalls' regiment and your Brother, Clinton's because I know it is the opinion of Genl Washington and the Board of War to whom that opinion was given that promotions should in common be regimentally but that that rule should give way in extraordinary cases.
> Rutledge to Livingston, Livingston Papers, NYPL.

❧ 5 ❧

Philip to George Clinton.
Papers of George Clinton, II, 843–845.

Camp, Valley Forge, Feb'y 13, 1778.

Sir,

About the 12th of Jan'y last, (after Hutting my men) I made application to his Excellency Genl. Washington, for lieve of absence in Order to Settle the accounts of my regt. and to purchase Clothing for my men, but Could not obtain lieve as Colo. Weisenfels was absent.[1] Since his Return three days ago, I apply'd again and was put off untill the New Regulations of the army takes place, which the General Informs me will be in a few Days but as it is uncertain when I Shall obtain a Furlough, must beg lieve to Request of your Excellency to order the Clothing (or a part), now in your State Store, to be sent to Camp for the 2d and 4th York Regts; for it is beyond Description to Conceive what the men Suffer, for want of Shoes, Stockings, Shirts, Breeches and Hats. I have upwards of Seventy men unfit for Duty, only for want of the articles of Clothing; Twenty of which have no Breeches at all, so that they are obliged to take their Blankets to Cover their Nakedness, and as many without a Single Shirt, Stocking or Shoe; about Thirty fit for Duty; the Rest Sick or lame, and God knows it wont be long before they will all be laid up, as the poor Fellows are obliged to fitch wood and water on their Backs, half a mile with bare legs in Snow or mud.[2]

Least your Excellency shuld Conceive I had not made timely application, I beg lieve to Observe, that I procured at Albany all the Clothing I Could get, which fell Short of what was wanting; as I Could git no Breeches, Shirts, Shoes, or Hats, I then Sent to the Convention for the articles wanting, but have Rec'd only thirteen pair Breeches, and Some Shoes, which are now worn out; this was all I got from them, Notwithstanding was Inform'd that Several Hund'd pair of Leather Breeches &c. &c. was Delivered to the Two Northern Regiments, who are in great want; it Scams to keep their Thighs from Scorching this winter in their warm Barracks.

I have made Repeated appplications and Sent Officers to no purpose. I am much at a loss to know the True reason of this neglect, but must Conclude they think us not Deserving; perhaps it may be said the Regiment is in debt and for that Reason will not Supply us—which to me is a very poor Reason, when they Consider in what manner I have been Imployed, and will further add that I was obliged to Defer the Settlement last Nov'r for want of Cash and time to do it. When I left Peekskill for this army I had Five months pay Due, which I have Rec'd at this place, and have made the proper Stopages for a Settlement which I do Intend Shall take place on my Coming up to the State—the Convention perhaps think, that a Regt. Continually on Command and actual Service, that has marched in one Campaign

Upwards of Twelve Hund'd Miles, Can at all times be Ready to pay their Debts and Settle their accounts, as well as those who lay in Quarters and always Ready to Receive their pay. However I know it has been Impossible for me to do it. I have much more to Say, but Shall not longer Intrude on your patience; Only beg lieve to Recommend me to your Self and good Family wishing you all Hapiness am with Great Respect,

Your Obt. Hum'l Ser't,
Philip Cortlandt.

[Addressed]
His Excel'y George Clinton
Governour State of New York.

---

1. Frederick Weissenfels was commissioned a lieutenant colonel in the 2nd New York on November 21, 1776. *D. Col. N.Y.*, XV, 138–139.

2. The extraordinary problems of supply, as reflected in the plight of the men under Van Cortlandt, compelled Washington to take a personal interest in revising the Quartermaster's Office. "New Regulations" were issued on February 5, by which that Office was to be reorganized. Nathanael Greene was then made Quartermaster General in March 1778. See Douglas Southall Freeman, *George Washington* (New York, 1951), IV, 541–633; Ward, II, 545–547; Rafael P. Thian, *Legislative History of General Staff of U.S. Army* (Washington, D.C., 1900), pp. 154–155.

✤ 6 ✤

George Clinton to Philip.
Papers of George Clinton, II, p. 845.

Poughkeepsie 4th March 1778.

Sir,

Before I received your Letter of the 13th Febry. ultimo I had given an order to Capt'n Ryker of your Regt., on the Commissary of Cloathing for the articles he returned wanted.[1] I am sorry however to Inform you that from the low state of the store as returned to me by Mr. Henry,[2] you will be able to receive but a very small proportion of the articles ordered (shirts excepted); the business of Cloath'g our Troops has hitherto been too much neglected. It is but within a few days since they have been in the least subject to my order and now indeed only in the Issuing of them. Measures are taking for acquiring a fresh supply, and I would fain hope the Troops will be soon better provided; and you may rest assured that however matters may have been hitherto mismanaged, I shall take care that an equal and fair Distribution of the Cloathing be made in the future among the Regiments. I am Sir with great regard Your Most Obed't Ser't

Geo. Clinton.

[Addressed]
Colo Cortlandt.

122

1. Captain Abraham Ryker (Ricker) was a close friend of Philip's. An epidemic which swept the camp at Valley Forge in May 1778 would claim Ryker as a victim. *N.Y. in Rev.*, p. 186; Philip to Pierre Van Cortlandt, May 7, 1778, p. 125.

2. John Henry served as Commissary of Clothing for the New York regiments. *N.Y. in Rev.*, p. 537.

⠂⊰{ 7 }⊱⠂

Philip to Pierre Van Cortlandt. ALS
NYPL

Camp Valley Forge May 7-1778

I have the pleasure of Informing you that I had
the Honour Yesterday of being present at & partaking
with the Officers and Soldiers of Our Army the Joys of
the greatest Day Ever yet Experienced in Our Independent World of Liberty-[1] A feu de Joy was Fired in the
Following Manner After the Troops were Arrived at
their posts which was on the high grounds formed in two
lines in Order of Battle. A Signal Gun being Fired at the
park was followed with a Discharge of Thirteen
Cannon—Fire'd on Our left near Schulkill a Running
Fire of musquettry then began On the Right of the Army
and so on from Right to left untill the whole Army had
Fire'd Then a Signal Gun and all the Army Gave Three
Huzza's for the King of France, Then Repeated in the
Same manner 13 Cannon a Running Fire and Huzza's
for the Friendly Powers in Europe the Same Fireing took
place with three Huzza's for the Free and Independent
American States—We then March'd Our Men to their
Respective Parrades and Dismis'd them Waited on his
Excellency where all the Officers of the Army had the
Honour of Dining under Sheds Cover'd with Tents for
that purpose—Our Army is in Exceeding fine Spirits and

124

a universal Joy Crown'd the Day[2] we hear from M.r How by Deserters which Come in Every Day from them that the Report in Philidel.a is that Congress has Agreed to Lord Norths proposal's—[3] and that there will be no more Fighting this is done I Suppose to prevent Desertion I have no more News to give you at present must therefore beg of you to make my Kind Love and Respects to Mamma Brothers & Sisters and Accept the Same from Y.r Dutifull Son Philip Cortlandt

May 10.th 1778—

Not having had an Oppertunity of Sending this letter untill now gives me an oppertunity of adding to it and to Observe how frail Mankind are and if it is the will of God but of Short Duration—When I Came to Camp which was the last of April I found all my Officers in Good Health Cap.t Riker among the Number who is now in Eternity he was taken Sick the 2.d of May went out of Camp the 3.d- Died the 8.th and was Buried the 9.th I herewith Inclose a letter to M.r Bradford his Brother in Law this his Sister May be made acquainted with the Death of Husband I had him Interred with the Honours of War in the Burying Yard of Valley Presbeterian Meeting About 3 Miles from Camp

I Rec.d yours by Lieu.t Fairlie who Arrived the Day before Yesterday Am Much Obliged by Your Advancing him Fifty Dollars—Am Very Sorry to hear of the loss of the Cattle what a Pack of Villains them Basley's are In my Opinion there is not One of them to be Trusted

Deserters from the Enemy are Daily

Coming in they say their Officers tell them the Fireing in Our Camp was Occasion'd by a Party of their's Attacking Our Camp—It is Expected that we Shall all keep Our present Situation at least four Weeks longer
My best Respects &c. from Y.r Dutifull and

Affectionate Son
Philip Cortlandt

[Addressed]
Pierre Cortlandt Esq.r

---

1. Unofficial news of the Franco-American alliance reached Washington's headquarters on April 30. He sought confirmation from Congress, but no word was forthcoming from them. At that point, on May 5, a copy of the *Pennsylvania Gazette* arrived containing the terms of the treaty. Washington then issued orders that

> It having pleased the Almighty ruler of the Universe propitiously to defend the cause of the United American States and finally, by raising us up a powerful friend among the princes of the earth, to establish our liberty and Independence up[on] lasting foundations, it becomes us to set apart a day for gratefully acknowledging the divine goodness and celebrating the important event which we owe to his benign interposition.

Quoted in James T. Flexner, *George Washington in the American Revolution, 1775–1783* (Boston, 1967), p. 289.

2. Philip celebrated the "universal Joy [which] Crown'd the Day," along with other officers who joined George and Martha Washington in a meal consisting of "a profusion of fat meat, strong wine and other liquors." *Ibid.*, pp. 290–291.

3. Lord North's three peace commissioners, William Eden, the Earl of Carlisle, and George Johnstone, reached Philadelphia in June 1778. By that date the decision had already been made to abandon Philadelphia to the American forces. The Continental Congress, furthermore, had rejected North's peace proposals with its stipulation that Americans continue to recognize Parliament's right to govern over them on April 22. Alden, pp. 386–387.

4. According to one of the standard genealogical references, Captain Abraham Riker of Newtown, Long Island married a cousin, Margaret Riker, in September, 1766. Cuyler Reynolds, *Genealogical And Family History Of Southern New York And The Hudson River Valley* (New York, 1914), II, 729.

5. James Fairlie soon became an aide-de-camp to General Steuben. Heitman, p. 221.

◦❦{ 8 }❧◦

Philip to John Jay.[1]   Dfs
NYPL

Rochester April 14, 1779—

Dear Sir

I herewith take the liberty to Inclose you a Petition to the Honourable Congress from Colo. Gansevoort and mySelf also a Certificate Signed by the Chairman and Several members of the Committee of Arrangement who arranged the officers of the Regiments Raised under the Direction of the State of New York which I beg may be laid before the Honl. Congress for them to Consider of and grant Such Relief as they in their Wisdom Shall Determine—Permit me likewise to Submit to your Consideration some Remarks I shall make with Respect to the Dispute Rank between me and Colo. Dubois—[2]

As soon as I was apprised of his appointmt. I Remonstrated against it in a letter Dated at Ticonderoga & Directed to the Convention of the State of New York, being Conscious that he had not meritted the promotion he had Received. Unless his Remaining in Canada was Sufficient when (as I am Informed) he was Induced so to do by Receiving a Brevet from Genl. Montgomery appointing him Major and would not Remain on any other Terms—Since his appointment as Colo. he has done no

128

more than his Duty and Scarcely that for it is well known he has been near half his time absent from his Regiment leaving the Commd. to a Captain; the other Field Officers being Prisoners—He has also broke the Faith he pledged to Your Excellency and the other Gentlemen of the Committee of Arrangement in Denying the facts which are Certified with Respect to acceeding the Right of Seniority to Colo. Gansevoort and mySelf and Still persists in Such Claim—I Conceive that when Congress Countermanded the Raising that Regt to which he was appointed they did in fact Revoke the Commission they had granted him for it appears that if the State had not given him an appointment he would have been out of the Service as was the case of Jo. Nicholson[3]—I should feel mySelf Exceedingly Injured Should Congress Establish his Rank Superior for it was my Determination Not to be Commanded by him, and had I not Received Such assurences when the Commission was offered me, which I have the Honour to hold by the Committee of which your Excellency was a member that Colo. Dubois was bound in Honour not to Claim Rank of me, I should not have accepted the Command. Nor Can I Submit to it now for I am assured he has no Right of Seniority over me—Is it not Exceedingly Unjust that he should Desire to take the advantage not only of me but of the Intentions of the Gentlemen who were Induced to do him Service who I am Confident would not have Indulged him if they had only Suspected that by so doing they would Deprive us of our right and place us in such a Disagreeable Situation as in order to do ourSelves Justice we should be obliged to Lieve the Service which for my part I shall be under the

Necessaty of doing however Disagreeable. The motives
which Induced me to Enter the Service you are not a
Stranger to and will Readily Conclude that a man who
has Sacrifised Domestick Ease for the Sake of Serving his
Country and to have an opportunity of Distinguishing
himself having Entred the Service at the Earliest period
of the War and Continued with the Applause of his
General near four Years must Experience the keenest
mortification upon such an occasion Not withstanding
my Prospects with Respect to accumulating Riches would
be greater out of the Service that in it is beyond a doubt
not to mention many other Considerations of Ease and
advantage yet I find that same Spirit which first actuated
me on Entering the Service Still Continues Relying on
your Readiness to promote Justice together with your
thorough Knowledge of the premisses I flatter myself
that upon a proper Representation to Congress of the
Facts In Question that the Difficulties will be Removed to
the Satisfaction of him who Remains with all Respect

Your Excellences Obt.
Humb. Sert,
Philip Cortlandt

[Adressed]
His Excellency John Jay
President of Congress

---

1. John Jay, friend, relative, and revolutionary associate of
   Philip's father, was then serving as President of the Conti-

130

nental Congress. It was to Jay that Philip finally turned in his frustration over his numerical rank in the Continental forces.

2. The matter of his ranking in the list of colonels had been a constant source of irritation since the New York government created an independent military command for Lewis DuBois in 1775. Not only did Philip and Peter Gansevoort feel slighted by the placing over them of a man whom they regarded as militarily inferior, but they felt that their own sacrifices were going unrewarded. Philip's petition was first referred to the Board of War and then to General Washington. The issue was resolved in June, 1779 when Washington determined that "Colonel DuBois rank in the line of the army of the U.S. of America after Colonel Van Cortlandt and Colonel Gansevoort." The petition dated April 9, 1779 can be found in No. 42, VIII, Folio 39 of the *Papers of the Continental Congress*. Entries concerning the petition are in Worthington C. Ford., ed. *Journals of the Continental Congress*, XIII, p. 490; XIV, pp. 510, 694.

3. John Nicholson served as captain under Colonel James Clinton in 1775 and 1776 and then was promoted to lieutenant colonel of a New York regiment during the Canadian campaign. He afterwards was put on detached service along the Hudson River. *N.Y. in Rev.*, p. 252.

◦⋄{ 9 }⋄◦

Philip to Pierre Van Cortlandt. ALS
NYPL

Camp Jacobs Plains, 13 Miles North of
Wyoming *Town* June 20–1779

Dear Sir

Since my arrival at this place[1] I had the pleasure of
receiving your's of the 8th Instant—I observed with
pleasure that Gilbt. & Van Wyck Very Luckily escaped
being taken I long to hear that S.ʳ Harrey has received the Beating which he will most undoubtedly have
upon Attacking the Fort.[2] I make no doubt but you have
the particular with respect to the success of Genl. Lincoln
in the Southern States I am Informed that he Totally
Defeited the Enemy killed and wounded upwards of
1400 most glorious News[3] and seems to give a Spring to
our Expedition which is not yet in forwardness enough to
move forward being delayed for the stoves and provisions coming up the Susquehana I have the pleasure to
Inform you that the arduous task I had in hand is Completed the road was Finished the 14th Instant being Just
one month in the Wilderness and Cut and Clear'd Near
Forty Miles many places Very Long Bridges and Cross
ways were made in the above time[4] I am Still on Detached
Command being the advance party at present with

Three Regiments under my Command being the Same I march'd to this place from the road. Viz. 2d, N.York Colo. Spencer and 1st New Hamshire Regts as the latter did not Join me untill I had near Finish'd ⅔ of the way—my camp is Situated in A Beautifull plain by the Side the Susquehana River which abounds in fish of Several Sorts. Pike and Rock are the best The land is good as far as I have been (which is Ten miles below this) a fine Intervale Country along the Banks of the River which Streak of land is from and Quarter to One mile wide in Each side in General and good upland to the Mountains which in many places are four miles from Each other—or 2 miles from the River. I am told that there was in what These people call the limits of Connecticut near Six Hundred Families before the Indian Drove them off last year[5]—We are now about 100 miles from Chimung the first Indian Town we shall attack; the River is Navagable near Sixty or perhaps 100 miles farther and all the way good land the low flats are as good as these on the Mohawk River. I fear perhaps I shall tire you with Reading this Long Discription of a Country you do not intend to Visit but I do assure you if you had lived as long among Pine Trees and Swamps as I had done previous to my arrival here you would have been in Rapture as was the Case with me when I came to the top of the mountain and beheld the Country it brought to mind the History of Old Moses when he was on Mount Pisgah the propect so beautifull and my Thoughts at that time so pleasingly Imployed that in the midst of midetations I quite forgot that I had ordered the Detachment to Rest them Selves and had it not been for my Major who Reminded me it was time to march perhaps I Should have been Rather unmercifull in the length of this letter especially if I had Committed to writing all the Remarks that I should have made—pray permit to Say a little more and I have done for this time—I forgot to mention the time we shall proceed up the River—it is Said in about 3 weeks as General Sullivan is still at Easton with the Army as they would only Distroy the provisions and thereby retard the march he therefore waits untill all is Ready—You Remember Wm. Hooker Smith I saw him yesterday his farm is about one mile from this he is now Imployed as a mate in the Hospital at the Fort. Jo. Depew is with the Indians he lived above this towards Tunkanunch—Old Traviss Brother to the late Joseph Travis of Peekskill Desired to be remembred to you—he lives near Fort Penn and Several other persons from York State—Our Troops are in fine Spirits and Exceeding Healthy I have but one Sick my [man] in my Regiment plenty of provisions and Again I think will do the Business for the Saviges of which articles we have enough as yet as this will in all probably be the last letter you will receive from me in some time please to make my best Love to mama and in a work to all where Due and the best Respects of your Dutifull Son

Philip Cortlandt—

P.S. Letter Can Come to me from Easton where perhaps I Shall not be able to send any to you. Therefore please to write when you have an opportunity.

[Addressed]
To Pierre VCortlandt Esqr.—

134

1. The Wyoming Massacre, during which some two hundred settlers had been killed by Indians, occurred in July 1778. This region is now within Pennsylvania and New York; Wyoming Town is now Wilkes-Barre. James T. Adams, *Dictionary of American History* (New York, 1951), V, 497; Alden, pp. 432–435.

2. Philip is apparently referring to Sir Henry Clinton's efforts at seizing the forts in the Hudson Highlands. Stony Point fell to Clinton's army on June 1, 1779. Its sister fortification, Fort Lafayette, fell soon after. Ward, II, 596–597.

3. General Benjamin Lincoln was on a successful march from the Savannah River in South Carolina to Augusta, Georgia, in the early months of 1779. His army won a series of confrontations with the enemy which was under the command of Augustine Prevost. *Ibid.*, pp. 684–685; Boatner, pp. 49–50, 1034.

4. Philip had been placed in command of a force whose task it was to clear a road from Easton to Wyoming, a distance of some sixty-five miles. Philip completed his portion of the road in thirty days. It was exceedingly dense country and it took extra efforts to create a military road. This was recognized by General Sullivan who thanked Philip and Colonel Oliver Spencer of the Fifth New Jersey Regiment for their "unparalleled exertions in clearing and repairing the road to Wyoming." Cook, p. 118.

5. Connecticut claimed lands in western New York and Pennsylvania based on grants issued to the Earl of Warwick, Lord Saye and Sele, and others, of land lying between the forty-second and forty-first parallels, and the

subsequent transfer of these lands to the Province of Connecticut. She continued to press these claims until 1800, when by an act of Congress, Connecticut's claims to lands in what is now Ohio (Western Reserve) were recognized provided that state relinquished her claim to lands within New York's and Pennsylvania's boundaries. Alexander C. Flick, ed., *History of the State of New York* (New York, 1934), IV, 116–117, 144–145. For additional information on Western Reserve see, Harold C. Syrett, ed. *Papers of Alexander Hamilton* (New York, 1973), XIX, 18, n. 33.

⚜ 10 ⚜

Philip to Pierre Van Cortlandt.   ALS

NYPL

Camp Near Wyoming[1] July 23d., 1779

Dear Sir

I have the pleasure of your Favour of the 30th last month Inclosing a letter from Gilbert[2] since which have Received the Agreable Account of Genl. Wanes success at Stony Point,[3] and beg to Congratulate you theron I am exceeding happy on Your Account and our Friends in your Quarter who I suppose were in some fear not knowing the Fate of war but I suppose all your Fears are now Vanished and of course in high Spirits I make no doubt but the Enemy will soon Sail for New York if they can make their Escape and then there best way will be to High for old England as fast as they can—we have the Acct. of the Enemies Success in N England but that like many of their past actions serve only as Blemishes Instead of addorning their Modern History[4]—I make no doubt you will be surprised to find we are yet at this place but so it is here we are still and here like to be these six Days and if (God Please) no longer I am Out of all Patience and so is our Commr, in Chief you may Suppose but you will ask pray why the Delay—I answer because a Set of Villains are permitted to live—would you believe that when I arrived at this post after making the Road, there was Provisions only from hand to mouth and all the Army coming on from Easton[5] after me Expecting that the Stores were arrived from Sunbury[6] which is 94 miles below this but Instead of the State of Pensylvania Send-

137

ing 700 men (besides Batteau men) I know but of Seventeen Inlisted those men were to act as Rangers with Genl. Hand,[7] the Commissaries of Purchases I believe to be a set of Villains I mean those who was to furnish this Army as appears from their Delays—and had it not have been for the most Strinuous Exertains of General Sullivan[8] and Genl. Hand before Sullivan came here the Expedition must have fallen through—we have Sent Soldiers down for provisions and Stores to Sunbury and to Easton all which will be in by Accounts in Three—days; an express goes off tomorrow to Genl. Clinton[9] I suppose with orders to march God grant us success and the War is at an End, in all Probibility—Our fair has been good hitherto to plenty of Beef and Bread and men Healthy—I am with my old Friend Genl. Poor,[10] so that our men are very Happy as they have Confidence in Each other and Call them Selves the fighting Brigade—my best Respects to all Friends to Colo. Livingston[11] in particular and your Neighbours Congratulating them on the good News and wishing they may have as good acctg. of us is the wish of your Dutifull Son—

Philip Cortlandt

[Addressed]
Pierre Van Cortlandt Esqr.

———

1. Although the name "Wyoming" was sometimes applied to a larger area in Pennsylvania, the Wyoming Valley of the Revolution was the 25 mile stretch of the Susquehanna River below the mouth of the Lackawanna River. Van Cortlandt was with Major General John Sullivan's expedition against the Iroquis in the Wyoming Valley. The pur-

pose of the expedition, which lasted from May to November, 1779 was to stop frontier raids launched from Canada by Tory and Indian forces. Gordon, *Gazetteer of the State of Pennsylvania*, pp. 493–396; Boatner, pp. 1072–1073, 1221–1222.

2. Gilbert died in 1786.

3. Brigadier-General Anthony Wayne of the Continental Army was commissioned on February 21, 1777. By an act of July 26, 1779, it was "Resolved unanimously, that the thanks of Congress be presented to Brigadier-General Wayne for his brave, prudent and soldierly conduct in the spirited and well-conducted attack on Stony Point; that a gold medal emblematical of this action be struck and presented to Brigadier-General Wayne." He continued to serve to the close of the war. He later became a Major-General and Commander of the United States Army, on March 5, 1792.

   The engagement took place on July 16, 1779. Stony Point, taken by the British June 1, was stormed and taken by an American force of 1,350 under Wayne. The American commander reported losses of 15 killed and 83 wounded. The British reported 20 killed, 74 wounded, 58 missing, and 472 captured. Boatner, pp. 1062–1067; Heitman, p. 577.

4. About 2,600 British troops under Sir Henry Clinton undertook a large-scale expedition in July 1779 to punish Connecticut for attacking British shipping in Long Island Sound and for supplying the rebel army. New Haven was entered and plundered, and Fairfield was occupied and plundered on the 8th. Boatner, pp. 260–261

5. Easton is 56 miles north of Philadelphia, and situated at the confluence of the Delaware and Lehigh rivers. The

main body of Sullivan's force, some 2,500 officers and men were assembled at Easton by the time Sullivan arrived on May 7. *Ibid.*, pp. 1072–1073.

6. Sunbury is on the east side of the Susquehanna River. Gordon, *Gazetteer of the State of Pennsylvania*, p. 434.

7. Brigadier-General Edward Hand of the Continental Army recieved his commission on April 1, 1777. He later became an Adjutant-General of the Continental Army.

8. Major-General John Sullivan had served earlier as a brigadier-general of the Continental Army. By an act of October 14, 1779, it was "Resolved, that the thanks of Congress be given to Major-General Sullivan and the brave officers and soldiers under his command, for effectually executing an important expedition against such of the Indian nations as, encouraged by the councils of his Britannic majesty, had perfidiously waged an unprovoked and cruel war against these United States, laid waste many of their defenseless towns, and with savage barbarity slaughtered the inhabitants thereof." Sullivan resigned on November 30, 1779. Heitman, p. 527.

9. Brigadier-General James Clinton was Governor George Clinton's brother. Clinton, having moved to Lake Otsego had written to Sullivan on June 30, and was awaiting orders from Sullivan to proceed to Tioga. Boatner, p. 1073; Heitman, p. 161.

10. Brigadier-General Enoch Poor of the Continental Army was commissioned on February 21, 1777. He had served earlier as the colonel of the 2d New Hampshire from May 23 to December, 1775, and then as colonel of the 8th Continental Infantry, *Ibid.*, p. 446.

11. Probably Colonel Henry B. Livingston.

140

⊶⊰ 11 ⊱⊷

Philip to [Gilbert Van Cortlandt]. ALS
NYPL

Tioga Augt. 22d, 1779[1]

Dear Brother

Your Agreable Favour of the 28 July Came to
Hand yesterday I am made exceeding Happy to find that
all our connections are well and do assure you that nothing gives me more satisfaction and Rest assured that
your Very Humble Servant is well and in good
condition—I am much obliged for your Extinsive Inteli-
gince with Respect to things communicated in your
Favour and now permit me in my turn to Inform you of
what has happened since I left Wyoming. (Previous to
that I have already Informed both you and our Honoured Favour [Father])—The Army left Wyoming the
31st July and arrived at this place the 11th inst. lay by one
Day and Sent Scouts to the town of Chemung[2] which
returning the 13th we were order'd to march leaving our
Camp and camp guards behind for the Sd. Town arrived
in the morning Just Day break the Distance 15 miles we
found the Enemy had deserted it upon which we plundered and Burnt the place consisting of about 30 Houses
and Distroyed fields of Corn to the amount of 2000
Bushels and Vast Quantities of Beans Squashes pumkins

141

&c—However an unfortunate Accident happen'd to A party advanced (who were gone to a town six miles farther up the Tioga Branch[3] on which Chemung stands) and were fir'd upon by the Indiands who lay in Ambusnade for them one mile from the town—the loss we sustained was two officers and ten men wounded and Seven killed what loss the Enemy met with is uncertain Several was seen to fall and were taken off by their party—this I hope will be a caution to our troops to racinetere [reconnoiter] the woods in their front better than they had done. At the time this happened I was in the town burning the Houses—we Return'd the same Day to this place and on the 15th was order'd together with a party of one Thousand men under the Command of Genl. Poor—to Reinforce Genl. Clinton who we met about 36 miles from this place Called Choconouch 7 miles west of Chenango[4]—and arrived here with him yesterday 11 oClock—The Day after tomorrow we proceed on the Expedition passing by the Town of Chemung which is already Destroyed and the next town is but 6 or 8 miles farther Then we Enter their Country and Shall live on Corn beans &c. in plenty we Intend penetrating Toward Niagara[5] but shall not attempt that place this Campaign for want of provisions having only a Sufficiency to Carry us into the Genesey Country[6] about 120 Miles N.W. of this place we Shall Distroy all before us that is of provisions and Houses—and I believe from the Disposition of the Troops that Should the Savages fall in our Hands they will have small Quarter[7]—The finest Fields of Corn I Ever saw and well Tended we find in this Country—I forgot to mention that General Clinton did not see any Enemy from Lake Otsago[8] to this place They having all fled towards the Country we are going to and I do apprehend if we are attacked it will be near Genecey at least 80 miles from here—The Country is Very fine along the River and I do Suppose that many parts of the Upland is Very good also but badly watered so that the Chief Settlement will be on the Rivers and Brooks of water—I do Expect if the Sagoes do not take of my Night Cap to See you in December unless we should be ordered on Some other Expidition by that time for by the first of October we must be in some Christian land again or Starve to death which we are Determin'd Shall not be the Case as long as we can walk and have pack Horses to Cut Stakes from—we have Lived like princes untill this time and shall for 5 or 6 weeks longer after that it will be Tough times unless we should meet better success than we Expect—I will now read what I have Scribbled and then go on—I have made out to read it my self and if you can I shall be happy tho I doubt it—please to make allowances for blunders—I have now given you a long pack of news and will only add that all our Troops are in Health—and for my Regt. in Particular I have scarce a Sick man in it—I Join Clintons Brigade tomorrow—Now for Compliments love Respects &c. &c. and as you know how to Dispose of those to the Deserving and where Due please to Distribute always bearing in mind that I shall ever remain your very Obt. and Senior Brother—

Philip Cortlandt

1. Tioga, Pennsylvania (now Athens, Bradford County), near the joining of the Susquehanna and Tioga Rivers, and the southern boundary of New York. Gordon, *Gazetteer of the State of Pennsylvania*, pp. 20, 450.

2. Chemung, Tryon County, New York (now in southeastern corner of Chemung County). Spafford, p. 161. The most important action of the Sullivan campaign was to take place there (another place name for the action is Newtown) on August 29, 1779. Cook, pp. 458–459.

3. The Tioga River is a larger western branch of the Susquehanna River and rises in Pennsylvania. Spafford, p. 315.

4. Chenango, then in Tryon County, New York (the village of Chenango-Point is now Binghamton, Broome County). Spafford, pp. 160–161.

5. Fort Niagara was in Tryon County, New York (now Niagara County), on the east side of the Niagara River at its entrance into Lake Ontario. It was fifteen miles below the great cataract of Niagara. This fortress was built by the French about 1725, passed into British hands by the conquest of Canada, and was surrendered by the British to the United States in 1796. Spafford, pp. 259–260.

6. The expedition of Colonel Daniel Brodhead, Continental officer, Pennsylvania, with six hundred men was supposed to join Sullivan's expedition at Genesee for an attack on Niagara, but for lack of adequate guides he turned back fifty miles short of that town. Sullivan started a withdrawal and burned Genesee. Alden, pp. 435–436; Ward, II, 643–644.

7. Washington had assigned Sullivan the mission of "total destruction and devastation" of the Iroquois settlements, specifying that the country was not to be "merely overrun but destroyed." At the end of the expedition, Sullivan reported the destruction of forty towns, "besides scattered houses," an estimated one hundred and sixty thousand bushels of corn, and "a vast quantity of vegetables of every kind." The civilization of the Six Nations never recovered from this blow although savage border warfare continued into 1780 and 1781. Barbara Graymont, *The Iroquois in the American Revolution* (Syracuse, 1972), p. 222; Cook, pp. 296–305.

8. Otsego Lake, situated in Tryon County, New York (now in Otsego County), sixty-six miles west of Albany. The Susquehanna flows from this lake. Spafford, p. 268.

❧ 12 ❧

Pierre Van Cortlandt to Philip. ALS
NYPL

Albany Feby. 8, 1780

Dr Son Philip

I have Received your Letter which you Intend'd for Gov.ʳ Clinton[1] and Let him have the Sight of it on which he desired me to Let some one of the Committee who where appointed to Report on the Subject matter of Cloathing and Providing Necessaries & cor for the Army See it.[2]

The Legislature have it now under their most Serious Consideration and you may depend that they will do as far as the Circumstances of this State will admit. The Great obsticall is the money. which I suppose will be raised from the Sale of the Confiscated Estates[3] Every member seems to be Realy Concerned. Knowing that unless the army is Supported what must be the Consequences. As soon as the Law passes for Supplying the army will send it to you pr first opportunity.[4] I have Lately heard from home your mother & all friends were well there Gilbt. is gone down with two Slays to Peeks Kill[5]

Have also Rec'd your Letter of ye 23 ultimo have observed the Contents and shall make the Best use of it to my friends that I Can

I hope this may find you in health and believe me to be your affectionate Father

Pierre Van Cortlandt

1. On January 23, 1780, James Black wrote to George Clinton from the "Camp near Morristown," that ". . . Breeches, Shirts, and Stockings, are most wanted. . . . Colonel Cortlandt informed me that he has transmitted to your Excellency an account of what the Troops of several states receive above the Continental allowance." *Papers of George Clinton*, V, 460.

2. A "joint Committee of the Senate and Assembly, appointed to report the Means proper for procuring a Supply of Provisions for the Army," reported to the Senate on February 3, 1780, "That the principal Complaint is with Respect to the Article of Bread" and recommended legislation for state assessors to "seize" wheat and flour for dispersal where it was needed. [New York State Senate], *Votes and Proceedings of the Senate of the State of New York, 3d Session, Commencing August 24, 1779, (Fish-Kill, 1779),* pp. 61–62.

3. In November 1779 a measure was adopted by New York which declared that "divers persons holding or claiming property within this State, have voluntarily been adherent to the said King, his fleets and armies, enemies to this State, . . . by reason whereof, the said persons have severally justly forfeited all right to the protection of this State, and to the benefit of the laws under which such property is held or claimed, and whereas the public justice and safety of this State absolutely require, that the most notorious offenders should be immediately hereby convicted and attainted of the offence aforesaid, in order to work a forfeiture of their respective estates, and vest the same in the people of this State. . . ." *The New York Journal, and the General Advertiser*, November 29, 1779.

4. Pierre Van Cortlandt, Lieutenant Governor of the State of New York, and President of the Senate, was present at the session during which was read "A Message from his Excellency the Governor to the Legislature, delivered to the Honorable the House of Assenbly, and by them transmitted to this Senate." Clinton's letter dealt with the "distressed Situation of our Army for Want of an adequate Supply of Provision," and transmitted letters on this subject from Major-General Heath, and others. It was *"Ordered*, that his Excellency's said Message be referred to the Committee of this Senate, appointed to meet the Committee of the Honorable the House of Assembly to report the proper Means for supplying the Army with Provisions." *Votes and Proceedings of the Senate, 3d Session, pp.* 65–66.

5. Peekskill, in Westchester County, N.Y. is some 40 miles above New York City on the east bank of the Hudson. The Manor of Cortlandt surrounded the town of Peekskill. Spafford, *Gazetteer*, pp. 166–278.

⚜ 13 ⚜

Philip to Pierre Van Cortlandt.   ALS
NYPL

Camp MorrisTown[1] March 22, 1780

Honb[l]. Father,

This being the first Letter I ever wrote you of it's
kind I hope will appoligise for its self, when you consider
the Extravigance of the Times the Trifling sum allowed
by Congress for my Services (considering the Depreciated State of our currency) The Rank I am under the
absolute Necessaty of Supporting (pay or no pay) is it to
be wondered that I should at last be obliged to Call for
assistance, it took a large Sum to purchase the Horses I
have and lately a Suit of Clothes and Expenses to and
from Philadelphia has laid me at Least Twenty Pounds
hard Cash below Par. I have not been any way Extravi-
gant nor have I purchased half the Necessarys wanting I
have been obliged to make use of other mens mony to
pay my way—so that I am obliged to Remain in camp
untill I can discharge those Debts therefore I have no way
left but to make applycation to you for Fifty Pounds
Hard mony or the value thereof with which sum I shall
save my Credit as I shall want the mony before I Leave
Camp wish that you could Send it me by the post or any
other way.[2] I am sorry to give you this Trouble and much

149

more that I am obliged to do it but as it is the only time this five years hope you will comply with my Request *and excuse the liberty I have taken.*

I have Just heard that Mr. Lewis Scott[3] has Letter from Congress to Genl. Washington Informing of the Arrival of the British Fleet at Charlstown.[4] I have writ to Van Wyck to Consult you wether you will be able to Send me the sum Need full or not if not I have Desired him to Settle my Acct in Company and to transmit me the Ballance. Exchange was Sixty at Philadelphia fallen since I came away to 50—Please to write me per first opportunity my best Respects where Due from your Obedient Son—

Philip Cortlandt

[Addressed]
Hon^l. Pierre Van Cortlandt Esqr.

———

1. Morristown, Morris Township, Morris County, New Jersey, is seventy-one miles from Trenton, and seventeen miles from Newark. Gordon, *Gazetteer of the State of New Jersey*, p. 186. Washington created winter quarters for the main army at a camp in the hills around Morristown in December 1780. It was a winter during which the soldiers endured hardships from the exceptionally severe cold. Ward, II, 611–613.

2. By 1780, it was estimated that forty Continental dollars equaled one Spanish dollar. The ones who suffered most from this wild inflation were the soldiers who were paid in

Continental paper currency. It is surprising that Philip had not written such a letter before this date. Alden, pp. 448–449.

3. Probably Lewis A. Scott, only son of the New York patriot leader, John Morin Scott. James G. Wilson & John Fiske, eds., *Appleton's Cyclopedia of American Biography* (N.Y., 1888), V, 437.

4. Charleston, South Carolina. The fleet under the British admiral Mariot Arbuthnot, which appeared at Charleston on February 10, 1780, furnished heavy artillery for the siege operations and helped win a British victory. Boatner, pp. 207–214.

⇥ 14 ⇤

Philip to Pierre Van Cortlandt. ALS
NYPL

Camp [Morristown] March 23, 1780[1]

Hon^d. Father

Since writing the Inclosed I have Received your letter of the 8th Feby am Glad to find that a disposition has at last taken place in favour of the Army of the State, I was at a loss to account for the Conduct of the Legislature and was Determined to leave the Service had they not sent the promisary Resolves but it appears they mean to make the Service more Respectable than heretofore which taken place I remain in Service if not I leave it Next fall. I am loosing ground fast and to live like a Vagabond and at same time supposed to live like a Gentleman in more than my Patriotism can put up with at this Day, there was a time I would have fed on—bread and water as I have done and was content the reasen, my Country I thought Virtuous and Approved my Services, now I find it the Reverse, I see men living in Luxury and seam as if bent on the Distruction of Everything Virtuous, their Grand object is gain and living in high life Dispising all those who cannot or will not live like themselves; from observation I will Venture to assert that unless the remedy is applyed in time of Danger it will not when the patient is Recovered. I forsee that should the army struggle to the last and be content with promises only they will starve at the end of the war, it is not a time to expect Favours when Men grow Proud and Haughty the Danger over they will say pray who are those men you call officers or at least a great Majority pray what was they, let them Return to their Old Imployment and Support themselves as we do we shall then be thought useless beings and shall receive similar treatment the old pack Horses did on the western Expedition and what is truly mortifying the foremost of this Class I am Describing have made Fortunes at our Expense and have arose from nothing—but now you find them men of Importance for what Reason. Why a most powerfull one which is Riches and which will cause them to be Canvassed. I have lost already in the Service of my Country five years of the bloom of Life, and for what I know perhaps grow Old in it. was I to Continue to the End of the War, that is old in Constitution therefore it is become a most Serius Subject with respect to myself and I cannot help Reflecting on future Events Should I now leave the Service I have youth enough in my side to make some provision to Support myself thro life—but should I continue in the army I may set down at the end of the war and Curse my Folly. A Sweet Consolation truly, that my great patriotism should Reduce me to Begery—No my Dr. Sir I am Determined to have Something for something I will not be Content with promise Only—

I beg to Ask one simple Question. Pray if the Legislature mean Candidly to make Restitution to their troops why do they not pass a Law for that purpose, is it because their Finances is small Shurely that cannot be assign'd as a sufficient Reason—it rather in my opinion is a reason why they should remove the Doubts which will arrise in the minds of their Troops, for if I think a man has no Capital I will not trust him if I know his Estate is good I will take his bond and mortgage when I will not be satisfied with his promise only or as is the present Case the word of a Tenant at will The next owner says I made no such promise—

Now I believe your present Finances are small but I know your Capital to be good therefore pass a Law that such provision shall be made and at such time as you may conceive proper but at any Rate let us know what it is to be I am tired of hearing (That We will Remember your Services) pray who makes the promise a man or Set of men in office to Day tomorrow Out and not in again fore is it not absurd that I Should take A's promise that B will pay me mony when A does not know B nor never has or perhaps never will see him; let the Legislature act as Candidly with their Troops as I have Expressed my Sentiments and I will be satisfied I have the Disposition to Serve my Country that I had at first upon the above Conditions which I believe is the Sense of all the officers but I declair I have not Sported my Sentiments among them nor do they know them to this Day—

Hoping that you will please to Use your Endeavour to Comply with the Request made in the Inclosed I subscribe myself with all Respect to You and the Gentlm. of my acquaintance (Hoping you will excuse the length of this letter) your Dutifull Son—

Philip Cortlandt

[Addressed]
Pierre Van Cortlandt Esqr.

1. Philip's bitter letter from Morristown reflected the sentiments of the majority of men who struggled to survive the
coldest winter of the war. Since Valley Forge has been
ingrained in history as the epitome of suffering, it is
difficult for most to realize that the Valley Forge experience was a pleasurable one compared to the one at Morristown. Along with the cold came a lack of food and supplies,
and a marked decrease in their pay as a result of inflation.
The army subsisted on one-third rations while prices
skyrocketed. According to Ward, a horse cost twenty
thousand dollars in Continental dollars while a captain's
monthly pay was worth only thirteen dollars in hard currency. It is no wonder that this letter is marked with such a
tone of bitterness.

In October, 1780 the New York State Legislature
adopted a comprehensive measure to "liquidate and settle
the accounts of the troops of this State in the service of the
United States." By this Act, military officers, such as Philip
Van Cortlandt, were to receive promissory state certificates for eventual reimbursement of their back pay
which had rapidly depreciated. These certificates entitled
the holder to claim at the close of the war a monetary sum
covering his pay plus "interest for the same at the rate of
five per cent per annum from the date thereof." Many
soldiers were still attempting to collect their back wages in
1784. Ward, II, 612, 615; [New York State], *Laws of the
State of New York. . . . Sessions of the Legislature Held in* 1777,
1778, 1779, 1780. . . . (Albany, 1886), I, 298–303; Roberts,
I, 12–13.

THE YORKTOWN CAMPAIGN

The victorious American campaign which culminated in Lord
Cornwallis' surrender was a joint action in which the combined American and French armies under Washington and
Rochambeau eliminated the major English army in America
(page 156).

THE NEW YORK HIGHLANDS

The Second New York Regiment spent a great deal of time in
the region contained in the map (page 156).

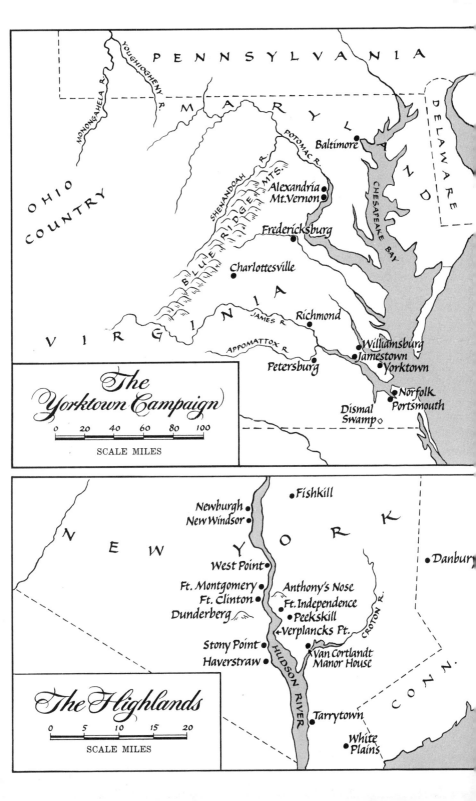

PENNSYLVANIA

MARYLAND

OHIO COUNTRY

VIRGINIA

DELAWARE

MONONGAHELA R.

YOUGHIOGHENY R.

POTOMAC R.

SHENANDOAH R.

BLUE RIDGE MTS.

CHESAPEAKE BAY

Baltimore

Alexandria
Mt. Vernon

Fredericksburg

Charlottesville

JAMES R.

Richmond

APPOMATTOX R.

Petersburg

Williamsburg
Jamestown
Yorktown

Norfolk
Portsmouth

Dismal
Swamp

The Yorktown Campaign

0   20   40   60   80   100

SCALE MILES

NEW YORK

Fishkill

Newburgh
New Windsor

Danbury

West Point

Ft. Montgomery
Ft. Clinton
Dunderberg

Anthony's Nose
Ft. Independence
Peekskill
Verplancks Pt.

CROTON R.

Stony Point
Haverstraw

Van Cortlandt
Manor House

HUDSON RIVER

CONN.

Tarrytown

White
Plains

The Highlands

0   5   10   15   20

SCALE MILES

-·⚜{ 15 }⚘·-

Philip to General James Clinton.[1] ALS
New York State Library

Fort Harkiman[2] June 5, 1781
Sir,
The first Convoy of Boats arrived at this place
yesterday and will set off again for Schuyler[3] tomorrow
morning and from Report will be able to bring off the
Remainder of the Garrison—I wish you to particularize
what number of pieces of Cannon[4] the Size and Quantity
of amunition[5] to be sent Down to Schenectady, the powder had best be sent by Land in Close Carriages[6] the
Roads will answer on this Side the River the Bridges
being made up-
Franks Hill[7] is a Short half mile from this and not 1 ½
mile as you supposed—I wish to have further Directions
what is to be done and in what manner—it will also be
Necessary to inform that if it is intended to build a Regular work[8] to Contain a Garrison of four or five Hundred
men that there should be provided without loss of time a
large number of Artificers[9] Provisions & Stores of Different Sorts too tedious to mention & a Quarter master and
Engineer[10] should be sent up immediately—if any Regiment is to Remain at this post[11] I wish Capt. Duboys to
join me—
Please to turn over

I beg lieve to propose the following plan—which considering our present abilities will in my opinion be most

157

advisable—it is to Erect a work calculated to Contain one Hundred men Constructed after the same manner as the work on Verplanck point[12] only with this Difference I would have a Barbet Battery[13] in such manner as to mount Cannon within the Work to have only Barracks Bomb proof with a Ditch pickets and Glacis[14] which will Effectually Serve it against Surprises and can be taken only by Regular approaches this Work will Command all the flatts[15] the River and as many Houses as the Inhabitants will want to Erect at the foot of the Hill towards this place[16] and Should you want to keep more men in this Quarter for Instance my Regiment they will be secure Enough in Camp. the above plan may be put in Execution and completed but if you Build a larger Work such as mentioned before you will want one Thousand men all this summer—I send this for your Consideration please to let me know your Sentiments on the Subject—perhaps you may think that a work upon the Construction I mention to Contain fifty Infantry and Twenty five Artilery may answer the purpose—

I am Sir your Hum^e. Ser^t.
P. Cortlandt

P.S.

I want a Close Carriage to keep Amunition in for the Use of my Regiment and the small Field Piece—
I hope it will not fall to my Lott to have my Reg^t. in Fatigue this Summer and Col^o. Willets[17] Levies to form a

flying Camp[18] as is Reported I Rely more on your better
Judgement than to suppose a thing of the kind

[Addressed]
Brig^r. General J^s. Clinton; Albany

---

1. Having seen action against Indians and Tories as the
leader of a western New York march in conjunction with
General Sullivan in 1779, Brigadier-General James Clinton was in command of the Northern Department after
1780 with headquarters in Albany. Here he remained until
Washington completed plans for the march south in the
summer of 1781.

When Washington appointed Clinton to take command at Albany, he added, "You will be particularly attentive to the post of Fort Schuyler and do every thing in your
power to have it supplied with a good stock of provision
and stores; and you will take every other precaution the
means at your command will permit, for the security of the
frontier. . . ." Fitzpatrick, XX, 259–260; DAB, IV, 229.

2. Although the name was spelled in different ways Lossing,
Pictorial Field Book, Vol. I, p. 255, gives an early spelling as
"Herekheimer" and Nathaniel Benton, *A History of Herkimer County* (Albany, 1856), p. 53, offers a spelling as "Har-
kemeis," this was Fort Herkimer, N.Y. It was located in
German Flats, Tryon County (now in Herkimer County), 5
miles south of Herkimer and 75 miles from Albany along
the Mohawk River. The inhabitants of German Flats,
which took its name from the fact that the first settlers were
of German origin, were remembered as having suffered
much in the Revolution.

Fort Herkimer was the large stone mansion of the
Herkimer family which was stockaded. In later years, the

JUNE 5, 1781

stones of this fort were used in the construction of a lock for the nearby Erie Canal and Fort Herkimer became "a prey to public vandalism." Lossing, *Pictorial Field Book*, I, 254; Spafford, *Gazetteer*, p. 194.

3. Fort Schuyler, N.Y. (now in Rome, Oneida County) was located at the head of navigation of the Mohawk River, and at the portage place between that river and Wood Creek, which led to Oswego. On this site of key importance to all of western New York, the French had built a fort to further their Indian trade. The British gained control of the area and built Fort Stanwix there. By the time of the Revolution, the fort was in disrepair and Colonel Elias Dayton, under orders from General Philip Schuyler, erected a fort which was called Fort Schuyler in honor of the general. "It has been confounded by some with Fort Schuyler, which was built in the French wars, near where Utica now stands, and named in honor of Col. Schuyler, the uncle of Gen. Schuyler," but there was no fort there at the time of the Revolution. William Campbell, *Annals of Tryon County* (New York, 1924), pp. 59–60.

The remote situation of Fort Schuyler meant that little protection from this fort could be given to the German Flats region of the Mohawk Valley against Tory and Indian attacks, such as the Indian invasion in 1778.

In May 1781, the destruction of Fort Schuyler by heavy rains and fire led to its abandonment and the withdrawal of the garrison to German Flats. The convoy of boats mentioned by Van Cortlandt in this letter to James Clinton was aiding in the evacuation of Fort Schuyler.

After the evacuation, Van Cortlandt records in his *Memoir* that he "destroyed all the fort. . . ."

4. To better understand the contemporary meaning of the many military terms used by Philip Van Cortlandt in this

letter, several sources can be consulted. The *Oxford English Dictionary* is the standard reference work for the ever changing definitions of English language words. A contemporary British text printed during the Revolution and popular with the American colonists was Thomas Simes's *Military Guide for Young Officers* published in London in 1776, and reprinted in Philadelphia the same year. Although William Duane's *A Military Dictionary* (Philadelphia, 1810) was published after the Revolution, it provides the most extensive military usage of the terms. Duane copied some definitions verbatim from Simes, which shows, perhaps, how little military terms changed before the age of mechanization. A brief glossary of military terms is included at the end of the second volume of Ward's *The War of the Revolution*. Boatner's *Encyclopedia of the American Revolution* is also quite helpful in understanding military terms as used in the Revolution.

Cannons, or weapons with metal tubes, took their names from the weight of the ball they discharged. A piece that discharged a ball of 24 pounds, for example, was called a 24-pounder; one that fired a ball of 12 pounds was called a 12-pounder.

The mobile guns of the Continental Army were usually bronze and ranged from 3- to 24-pounders, with 5½- and 8-inch howitzers. A few iron siege guns of 18-, 24-, and 32-pound caliber were available.

For transportation, cannons were moved by horses or oxen, driven by hired civilian drivers.

For ammunition, cannons of the Revolution used round shot, grape, and case shot. Howitzers, short cannon, and mortars fired bombs and carcasses.

5. Ammunition was considered by Simes as not only bullets, cartridges and bombs, along with cannons and guns, but "all sorts of offensive and defensive weapons." It would include firelocks, bayonets, and swords, "and every thing

that may add to the destruction of the enemy, or your own preservation."

Schenectady had been a regular army post until the spring of 1780, when orders were given in March by the Board of War to discontinue this post and others because of the cost. Willis T. Hanson, *A History of Schenectady during the Revolution* (Privately printed, 1916), p. 102.

6. Ammunition and powder were loaded in carriages or wagons for transport. Exactly what "Close Carriages" were, is not certain, but Duane mentions a "Close bodied Ammunition caisson" without defining it in a list of carriage types. He defines a caisson as a covered wagon to carry supplies or ammunition.

   Both Simes and Duane define an ammunition cart as "a two-wheel carriage with shafts; the sides of which, as well as the fore and hind parts, are inclosed with boards instead of wicker-works."

7. There was a Frankfort Hill, in an area settled before the Revolution, near German Flats. It was on the south side of the Mohawk River, and on the same side as Fort Herkimer. Disturnell, *Gazetteer*, p. 172; French, *Gazetteer*, p. 344.

8. As Van Cortlandt described the task in his *Memoir*, he was "to build a new fort" at Fort Herkimer.

   An essential part of building the fort was the "works," or "the fortifications about the body of a place." Several lines and trenches had to be made around the area for security. This definition is in both Simes, and Duane, p. 747.

9. Artificers were soldier mechanics who made works or prepared ammunition such as fuses, bombs and grenades. The term "artificers" also applied to military blacksmiths, "collarmakers," and a particular corps in the army. Duane, p. 16.

The Continental Army had two artillery artificer regiments. One was commanded by Colonel Jedutham Baldwin and the other by Colonel Benjamin Flower. Heitman, p. 15.

10. Van Cortlandt's engineer at Fort Herkimer was Major Villefranche, according to the *Memoir*. Before becoming a major in the service of the United States in 1777, Villefranche had been a Lieutenant in His Majesty's Dragoons in France. Villefranche was described as an intelligent and exact person. He scattered all his fortune in America and obtained a pension of £500. Heitman, p. 667.

Of tremendous importance to military science and strategy in this period, the engineer was the officer who built or repaired forts, and set up defenses and offenses. Duane, *Military Dictionary*, pp. 136–137.

11. A post was a military station. The term meant "any sort of ground fortified or not, where a body of men can be in a condition of resisting the enemy," and could have applied to where Van Cortlandt's men were before the new fort was built. Duane, *Military Dictionary*, p. 542.

12. At the end of a peninsula of gently rolling land, Verplancks Point, Westchester County, N.Y. was on the east side of the Hudson River, some 42 miles north of New York City and 4 miles south of Peekskill. In 1788, Verplancks Point was contained in the area of Cortlandt Township, named for the original patentee. French, *Gazetteer*, pp. 698–699.

On the brow of the point, "near the western extremity and overlooking the water, a small fortification, called Fort Fayette, was erected. It was an eligible site for a fort. . . ." Along with the fortress of Stony Point on the opposite side of the river, the fort on Verplancks Point commanded the channel and Kings Ferry, the key crossing place between New England and the south.

163

Fort Fayette, also known as Fort Lafayette, was a small, complete work, unlike the fort at Stony Point which was unfinished in 1779. Fort Lafayette was enclosed "with pallisades, a double ditch, chevaux de Frize and abbatis, and had a block-house in the centre, which was bomb-proof. . . ." C. Stedman, *A History of the Origin, Progress, and Termination of the American War* (Dublin, 1794), II, 15; Lossing, *Pictorial Field Book*, II, 174–175.

After the British took the fort on June 1, 1779 it was demolished, and a "large, substantial one built in its stead, well mounted with artillery, and strongly garrisoned."

13. A barbette battery "in gunnery, is when the breast-work of a battery is only so high, that the guns may fire over it without being obliged to make embrasures: in such cases, it is said the guns fire *en barbette.*" A battery was a place of defense, as a mound of earth covered with green sod, where cannon or other guns are mounted to fire over a breast-work. A battery was usually about 8 feet high and 18 to 20 feet thick. Duane, pp. 33, 36.

Fort Lafayette on Verplancks Point had a barbette battery close to the blockhouse, and another barbette some distance away, according to a 1779 sketch drawn by Colonel Rufus Putnam. Henry P. Johnston, *The Storming of Stony Point on the Hudson* (New York, 1900 reprinted 1971) p. 223.

14. To protect the outskirts of the fort from the enemy, Van Cortlandt suggests that pickets, or sharp stakes sometimes shod with iron, be put up. Duane, *Military Dictionary*, p. 523.

Ditches were another means of fortification, "to the end that a small number of men within may be able to defend themselves for a considerable time against the assaults of a numerous army without. . . ."*Ibid*, pp. 126, 171.

A glacis was a bank sloping away from a fortification to

help defend it against attacks. "Some authors think these works never answer the expence," comments Duane. But, he continues, at least one authority thought them useful when the ground was right, "because, when such works are defended by a skilful governor, they will afford the means of being valiantly supported." Duane, *Military Dictionary*, p. 177.

Boatner, explains that because of the great labor involved in clearing timber and grading the soil to make the slope, a glacis was usually found only around permanent fortifications. Boatner, p. 436.

Van Cortlandt refers in his *Memoir* to the hard work of "clearing off the timber and brush. . . ."

15. As its name suggests, German Flats was surrounded by extensive alluvial flats. The soil on this wide plain was considered remarkably rich. Spafford, *Gazetteer*, pp. 193–194.

16. Around the stockaded stone mansion of the Herkimer family and a nearby church, the farmer's homes were clustered in order to have some protection from Indian and Tory attackers. Because of these threats, the farmers dared not live in isolation. There were some thirty-four homes and as many barns in this settlement, and about an equal number around Fort Dayton. Lossing, *Pictorial Field Book*, I, 254–255.

17. Long an active Revolutionary leader in the Mohawk Valley region and having distinguished himself in a successful sortie at Fort Stanwix during the St. Leger expedition of 1777, Marinus Willett was first appointed as lieutenant-colonel and later colonel of the 5th Regiment of New York. When the five New York regiments were consolidated into two units in 1780, Colonel Willett took command of the regiment of levies on the Tryon County frontier.

By July 6, 1781, Willett was at Fort Herkimer and on that date he wrote Washington: "I heartily wish to have as much force as possible, to assist in the preservation of a people, whose sufferings have, already, been so exceeding great." He said he would fix his quarters at Canajoharie because of its central position. Willett, *Narrative*, p. 76; DAB, XX, 244–245. Also see an extensive biography by Howard Thomas, *Marinus Willett: Soldier-Patriot* (Prospect, New York, 1954) which provides good coverage for this period of Willett's career; Frederick L. Bronner, in "Marinus Willett," *New York History*, XVII (1936), 273–280, offers a brief description of Willett's expeditions against the Indians and Tories at Sharon Springs in July 1781, and near Johnstown and Canada Creek in October 1781.

18. A flying camp was a body of soldiers kept in constant motion to provide a force quickly where needed and to keep the enemy in alarm.

In a letter to Washington, dated Fort Herkimer, July 6, 1781, Willett shows that Van Cortlandt's displeasure concerning the rumor that the Levies would form a flying camp did not change his strategy. Willett wrote: "I propose, as far as I can make it any way convenient, to guard the different posts by detachment, to be relieved as the nature of the cause will admit. . . . Having troops constantly marching backwards and forwards through the country, and frequently changing their route, will answer several purposes, such as will easily be perceived by you, sir, without my mentioning them." Willett, *Narrative*, p. 77; Duane, p. 77.

Philip to Pierre Van Cortlandt.   ALS
NYPL

Baltimore Sepr. 15, 1781[1]

Hond. Father

This is the first opportunity I have had since I left
Kings ferry of writing to you therefore beg you will
please to Excuse what you had a Right to Conceive
Neglect—

I arrived at this place Thursday last and have been
Joind since by the first Regiment General Clinton is also
here we shall embark tomorrow for Williamsburgh
which is I suppose by this time Head Quarters as General
Washington left this Six or Eight Days past the french
army march'd this morning by land from this Town for
Anapolis which is about 30 miles distant General Lincoln
was at the last mentioned place with the light Infantry
Jersie Brigade Hazens and the artilery—they have been
detained waiting for the French Fleet to Return which
put out the other day after the English who are gone off
& the French return'd as the Baren DeViominil[2] was
informed last Evening—so that General Lincoln will now
proceed as we shall with all Expedition—it is said
Cornwallis has made some proposals to the Marquis
LaFeitte which were Rejected he is compleatly hemed in

or will be in a few days in such manner as not to be able to Execrate [extricate] himself—he has a fine Position and is Very Industrious in fortifying himself & it is supposed that he will make an abstinate defence in hopes of Relief—he has near Six Thousand men Including 2000 Neagros & Torys. I think we are in a fine way of making them all prisoners of war Either Dead or alive—Our Army is Healthy and in good Spirits my Regiment in a Particular Manner and have been Very Fortunate in not loosing any men by Desertion except Three or four Drunken fellows which remained at Philadelphia those I expect to git again—I make no doubt considering our present prospects that this will be the last Compaign this War but should Britain still be obstinate the next must prove the Distruction of their Nation—The French Fleet Captured the Robuck Frigate and Several Transports[3] —one of which is now in the Harbour and my men are unloading her to proceed down the Bay with, she was loaded with Rum Sugar & dry goods—if we should be so fortunate as to have a fair wind we shall not be more than two days going down the Bay so that by the latter End of the week I expect to have a Sight of the British Works—

God grant success and that I may be so happy as to meet you all again in Health is the wish of your Dutifull Son—

P. Cortlandt

[Addressed]
Pierre V.Cortlandt Esqr.

1. General Washington began the preparations for a campaign against Lord Cornwallis in mid-August 1781. By August 21 the army was on the march. Philip refers in the *Memoir* to the maneuvering of his troops at that time so as to confuse Gen. Henry Clinton at New York. Some two thousand troops were engaged in this move from New York by way of New Jersey to the southern theater. From Baltimore, where Philip arrived on September 13, the troops later embarked on board transports and sailed for landings along the James River near Williamsburg, Virginia. Ward, II, 883–885.

2. Philip's spelling, which was always variable, played havoc with foreign names. Mentioned in this letter are: Baron deViominil—Lt. Gen. Chevalier DeVioméÁil and LaFeitte—Lafayette.

3. The decisive naval battle for the control of the Chesapeake occurred on September 5. A superior French force under Francois-Joseph-Paul, comte de Grasse assumed control of the Bay after a naval engagement with a British fleet under Admiral Samuel Graves. The *Roebuck* was a British frigate with forty-four guns. See Charles O. Paullin, *The Navy of the American Revolution* (Cleveland, 1906), pp. 207–208, and Harold A. Larrabee, *Decision at the Chesapeake* (New York, 1964), pp. 184–223.

·⋙{ 17 }⋘·

Philip to Pierre Van Cortlandt. ALS
NYPL

Camp before York Oct.ʳ 16 1781[1]

Dear Sir

My last to you was the day before we began to
break Ground, since which we have advanced our Second parrellel so as to Include Two Redoubts of the
Enemy which were taken the Night before last by As-
sault, with Very little loss on our part, one of them was
taken by part of our light Infantry led on by Lieu.ᵗ Col.º
Hamilton who commanded them the other was taken by
the French; we took (most of which were wounded with
the bayonet) upwards of Sixty men, and Killed a Number
how many I do not know; I was on Cam.ᵈ with the Brigade
since yesterday 12 OClock in the lines which is now not
more than 150 yards, and in some places not so far from
their Works and Batteries, so that we are Within Musket
shott of Each Other we were hard at work all last Night
Erecting Batteries, which will be ready to play on them
early tomorrow Morning when we shall make the Town
of York warmer than ever one was known to be in america; Our Right hand Battery only will consist of —(as
General Knox Informed me yesterday) 8. 24 Pounders
4—18 Pounders 2. large Hornits and Eight Morters of

170

10^S and 13 In.—besides several other Small Batteries; the Grand French Work in which I suppose will be 30 pieces of different sorts of Cannen & Morters Exclusive of other works so that in a few Day's we Expect to knock their works and Town and Town about their Ears—after Which if Cornwallis does not think proper to ask Quarter I suppose we shall advance on him with Bayenets fixed to the tune of Quick time—

His Excellency has not as yet (nor do I believe will) summen Cornwallis to Surrender so that the haughty Brittain if he wants Quarter will be obliged to ask it; which will be a most humbling stroke indeed—

from the Right of our line which is the Redoubt taken from them you have a fine Prospect of their works, Town of York, Shippen and Town of Gloster, which is oposite to York and is their Hospital it is thought by some that they will cross over to that place which may prolong the Seige five or Six days—but it is not my Opinion for he has not small Craft enough to take his army over without our discovering of his movement and in that Case he will—Sacrifise a large part of his men in the Attempt—I will Inclose you a small sketch of their Work, and Our line which I have only from Observation however it give you some small Idea of them

We took a Major and two Officers in one Redoubt what officers were taken by the French I do not know I have lost Two Men Killed and Three wounded of the Second Reg^t and as many of the first which is but Trifling considering how much they are often Exposed in maker Works and advancing on the Enemy—

I forgot to mention that the Enemy made a Sally with

171

the Hundred men at day brake this morning they fell in with our Sister Battery which was making but no Cannon Mounted only laying on the Ground several of which they spiked with the End of their Bayonets but Not to do them any damage for before they had the work one Minute the French Pushed them Out again with Bayonets Killed Ten on the Spot and wounded Several & Took Eight priseners they then ran for their works the french lost Two men Killed and Several wounded and one Officer—

Deserters are daily coming in from them who say they all Expect to be taken but Cornwallis tells them not he says he is shure the British Fleet will Relieve him for says he if we are lost the matter is Settled—

I agree exactly in that point with his lordship I am Very shure that the taken his Army (which is composed of their best Troops will have such Effect in Brittain that they will dispare of Ever Conquering us I must bid you adius with my Dutifull Respects I am Your's &c &c—

P. Cortlandt

---

1. See notes 54–63 to *Memoir*, pp. 91–93.

Index